Purpose in *Silence*

*Living in Silence but
Speaking Purposefully Through
Poetry and Devotional Writing*

TYRONE AND LYNDON BROWN

WESTBOW
PRESS®
A DIVISION OF THOMAS NELSON
& ZONDERVAN

WestBow Press books may be ordered through booksellers or by contacting:

WestBow Press
A Division of Thomas Nelson & Zondervan
1663 Liberty Drive
Bloomington, IN 47403
www.westbowpress.com
1 (866) 928-1240

ISBN: 978-1-9736-5566-4 (sc)
ISBN: 978-1-9736-5565-7 (hc)
ISBN: 978-1-9736-5567-1 (e)

Library of Congress Control Number: 2019902631

Print information available on the last page.

WestBow Press rev. date: 03/14/2019

Contents

Thoughts from the Heart

Dedicated to all those who worked to give us the confidence to write and especially Shirley Crawford (our education assistant) and Ruth Casanova (our Speech and Language Pathologist) who recognized our hidden abilities

Foreword

As parents we all wish the best for our children and trust that our hopes and dreams we have for them, before they are born, will one day be a reality. In our case, we have learned that "All things work together for good to them that love God" (Romans 8:28). When we received the first call from our doctor after having had an ultrasound of Tyrone, telling us that our child had clubfeet, we began on our journey with our two sons who have been a true blessing. We did not know what was ahead for us and Tyrone, and then two years later Lyndon, but without doubt our Lord has been with us every step of the way with strength and encouragement, only He can give.

Both Tyrone and Lyndon were born with clubfeet and a severe form of dyspraxia. Having clubfeet has been a tremendous trial for both boys, with several surgeries and much pain. The first surgeries Tyrone underwent were extremely painful, as his feet were opened up to lengthen ligaments and tendons, and afterward given only pain medication which normally is given for a tooth extraction. We will never forget, as he lay in the crib at eight months old, hearing him groaning from the severe pain. Lyndon also went through several surgeries and at present is waiting for further correction. When Tyrone and Lyndon speak of pain in their poetry, they write from experience.

The first years of Tyrone's and Lyndon's lives were very difficult, as doctors were unable to come to any specific diagnosis, and with slow physical development we were told they were mentally challenged. We were not given much hope for progress academically, and at one point were told "He's mentally challenged, pick your battles, no amount of medication will help this child." The frustration that both boys faced was extreme, as they had no way of communicating to us what they were actually thinking. Tyrone resorted to hyper-active behaviour and Lyndon to sleeping much of the time. Through it all we knew that the boys were far more aware of what was going on around them than anyone was giving them credit for. We believed in them, and more importantly believed our God was "able to do exceeding abundantly above all we can ask or think." (Ephesians 3:20)

At ages seven and five, respectively, we began taking the boys to a speech therapist (Ruth Casanova) who was the first one to give us hope and an understanding of what they were dealing with. She began therapy which proved their ability to spell and read. Her expertise was such a blessing to us and the boys as they finally were being given opportunity to prove who they truly were. With this knowledge Tyrone's education assistant (Shirley Crawford) began working on Tyrone learning to point to a laminated, paper keyboard and he began to write. Lyndon soon followed, as when it was understood Tyrone had certain capabilities Lyndon was given the same opportunities. It did not take long for us to realize the potential that was within these two non-verbal boys. However, not everyone was willing to believe it. Despite the doubters we believed in our sons and determined to give them every opportunity possible to progress and prove their intelligence.

When Tyrone was eight years old, his education assistant said to us, "You know that Tyrone is a speed reader." We had not realized that Tyrone had this ability and so we began to have him read the scriptures each night. He would scan down the columns of a chapter and we would then question him for the verse number for verses we would quote back to him. To our amazement we realized that he has a photographic memory. Of course we then worked on this with Lyndon and found that he also had this ability. The reading of scripture has played a major role in the knowledge and understanding they have of the Word of God. For both boys, faith and spiritual understanding have been their foundation and have kept them through their deep trials. Tyrone came to trust the Saviour at eight years of age and Lyndon at nine years of age. Trusting and praying motivates them to write for their Lord.

Striving to be understood and given opportunity during their early school years was the most difficult time for us as a family. As Tyrone and Lyndon are unique in their abilities and disabilities, they required an education fitted for their needs, with understanding and belief. However, the education system was not equipped for this and the boys struggled to be understood and accepted for who they are. There was much frustration and hurt so that eventually we were forced to home school them, with assistance from the school district. It was then that the boys began to rise above their label and prove their academic and writing abilities. Shortly after beginning their education with this partnership, they were encouraged to enter an essay in the Royal Commonwealth Essay Competition, for which they both won a prize in their category. The Lord was directing and answering prayer for our family and we were encouraged to work even harder at their education.

One memorable Sunday, which we will never forget, the late Mr. Ed Billingham spoke about Heaven and the wonderful reality that our frail bodies will be changed. Tyrone brought his IPAD to me afterward and said, "Mom, I'm so glad we believe we will be changed." We encouraged him to write a poem with these thoughts and so started to his poetry writing. Lyndon soon began writing poetry as well. We have combined their writings in this book, and it will become clear that they each have their own style of writing. Their poetry and writings are an expression of their faith in the Lord Jesus Christ, thankfulness for their blessings, their appreciation for God's creation and sharing their deep struggles which they have overcome.

This compilation of Tyrone and Lyndon's poetry and writings is truly a miracle and proof of God's purpose in trials. They have found hope in being special vessels, designed by God, to glorify His name and to make a difference in the lives of others who struggle with disabilities. Having purpose is what gives life meaning, and knowing God's purpose in one's life gives true meaning. For Tyrone and Lyndon they have found their purpose in writing and their desire is that through this the Lord Jesus Christ will be glorified.

Melody Brown

Preface

Tyrone Brown

Learning to trust my Lord and Saviour is the basis of my poetry and writings. Throughout my life I have faced adversity and pain and it is only by God's grace and strength that I have overcome the constant battle of frustration and anxiety. Far surpassing the negative label and helpless diagnosis which doctors gave when I was young; my Lord has given me the ability to communicate through writing, with a voice which I trust will be a blessing to others. More than words on a page, my writing speaks to the amazing power and strength I have found in "Christ who pours His strength into me" (Phillipians 4:13).

The personal struggles I am continually facing stem from severe dyspraxia, which has meant I am non-verbal and motor impaired. "Non-verbal" seems to translate into "mentally challenged", by most of the world, and has frustrated me more than words can express. With so much turmoil within the psychological impact has been anxiety. Perhaps this continual fight is greater than the dyspraxia itself. However, with prayer and faith I have been able to succeed in many areas of my life and especially writing, which I want to share.

Undoubtedly, having thoughtful times in meditation of the peace which God alone gives, my theme that is often found in my writings, is the power I have to overcome the negative thoughts that drag me down. Reflecting on "the peace of God which passeth all understanding" (Phillipians 4:7), my thoughts are protected from doubt and uncertainty. Without speech there can be misunderstanding, which poses incredible fear with frustration. However, each thought of peace brings the answer to my problems, with the Word of God my absolute assurance.

Testing and trials through life are more than tools to teach patience, but are the purpose of God to channel our life to become like Christ. My struggles are God's way of making my life have purpose, which is preparing me for eternal worship.

Tyrone Brown

Lyndon Brown

Since a child I have had struggles and misunderstanding, but God's purposes will prevail with all my weakness and disability. Each one of us is created to glorify God with the abilities He has blessed us with and my goal, through writing, regardless of my limitations, is that He will be given honour and glory. The writing of poetry is fundamentally a gift from my Lord, and it is my responsibility to write and share it with others. This is the primary reason for this book.

Learning to walk and talk is often taken for granted but in my case motor impairment has meant these physical responses have not developed as most. Walking is possible, but balance can be an issue, and speech is almost impossible. With having global dyspraxia, hand writing is also not a skill I can accomplish, so finding a way to communicate was difficult as a young child. In addressing my communication needs I have been able to overcome the stigma of being without thought because I am non-verbal. Unfortunately, without speech I was thought to be without intelligent thought or ability to learn, binding me in chords of frustration and discrimination. However, the Lord has purpose with all we are faced with and He has taken my weakness to prove His power in my life to overcome adversity.

Lyndon Brown

Purpose in Silence

Silently it rises, with purpose to shine in the night
Not lesser in purpose than the day's bright sunlight
Reflecting its light on the river it beams
Overcoming the darkness as the world around dreams
God created it by His word in power
Just as He created the beautiful flower
With purpose He takes what seems so weak
Boys with problems who cannot speak
Lesser they seem to many around
His purpose for them it does astound
Reflecting His glory; His plan for their life
Giving them strength through days of strife
Yet silence in voice will speak through words
The purpose of God within their hearts burn

Lyndon Brown

Devotions from the Heart

But seek ye first the kingdom of God and his righteousness; and all these things shall be added unto you. Matthew 6:33

Understanding that our life on earth is the foundation for our eternal destiny and the predetermination of our eternal blessing, will put into perspective what is really important in life. It is the requirement of God's righteous character that His Heavenly blessing given to his children, be in accordance to the righteousness of Christ. The first covenant was based on law and the living in accordance to the holy demands of God, but man failed miserably. The new covenant is through the righteousness of the Lord Jesus Christ and His perfect sacrifice. The difference now is that in believing we receive the Holy Spirit of promise, who will guide us into righteousness. However, we have a free will and it is incumbent upon us to live for our Saviour.

Promise with blessing is the founding truth of hope and faith. You and I are promised infinite blessings from our infinite God when we put Him first in our life. The happiness we find in our own successes is only for a moment in time, but the joy of the commendation of our Lord is eternal, with a crown of righteousness promised to those who love Him. Personal power to live the Christ centered life is through prayer and the Spirit of God being given the heart in submission to His will. Though fears and things of time may try to take hold of us, we must put our Lord and Saviour first, regardless of how the world may look at it. God's promise is His eternal blessing, spoken in the words of our Lord Jesus Christ.

Here I live with promise of eternal gifts in store
Seeking first my Saviour, the one whom I adore
The blessings unfathomable, as our God's heart of love
Infinite grace is the fountain, flowing from above
Not the things we strive for of life's fleeting days
Not the riches of this world or talents we display
Can ever have the value of God's eternal Son
Or the commendation of His words "Well done"

Tyrone Brown

"Behold I stand at the door and knock; if any man hear my voice I will come into him and will sup with him and he with me." Revelation 3:20

We do not always give our attention to a knock on our door, as calls from strangers are not always welcome, but in some instances the stranger is there to give us help or warning of danger in our neighbourhood. Through neglect or deliberate disregard of the knocking we may miss out on the opportunity for our good. Our Lord is standing at the door in hope of entrance, to be our companion and friend. Today is the time to open as He says "I stand", in the present tense. Time is of the essence. With His patience, in love He continues to knock at our hearts door that He might have acceptance and entrance into our life. The door separates us from the blessing God has for us and from forgiveness of sin, which is the promise He gives if we accept His gift. The hindrance that keeps us from opening the door prevents His salvation and hope being ours and from the joy that comes from having "a friend who is closer than a brother" (Proverbs 18:24). The persistent knocking is the patient grace and mercy of the God of love, who wants all to be saved (I Timothy 2:4), so that He can both have fellowship with us and bless us with His presence. The blessing is reciprocal, which is beyond our thought, that the God of Heaven would find blessing in saving sinners like me and you. The Lord Jesus Christ gave His life so that He can offer forgiveness of sin. The responsibility is ours to open the door and receive His offer of salvation.

He's Standing at the Door

In love He stands outside the door
He often knocks; He's been here before
Through grace He offers His gift to you
The choice is yours. What will you do?
Persistent He stands; He wants to come in
But the knob for the door is only within
Loud He knocks so you will hear
There's no excuse for a deaf ear
The one outside came from above
He is the one whose name is Love
Take heed to His knock ask Him to come in
His promise is, He'll save you from sin
The friend that never turns away
Who promises He'll always stay
Close by your side when all seems dark
His guiding hand your path He'll mark
The blessing is yours, but also is his
Communion together, when he in your heart lives

Tyrone Brown

Be still and know that I am God... Psalm 46:10

Our resource of strength is found in the stillness of God's presence. Note his command, "Be still". Having had considerable struggles throughout my life, and not having a voice, I know human weakness, but personal weakness has given me the realization that I am fully dependant on my Lord. Fighting a battle, I need the strength and leadership of a valiant warrior and captain who has a strategic plan that can conquer the enemy. Only the omniscient God knows the road ahead and the enemy's pitfalls that would seek to put me down. The Captain of my salvation commands me to "be still", and his promise is that he will pour his strength into me (Phillipians 4:13). The "being still" goes against the natural gratification of fulfilling my own desires. The tendency is to control my life's circumstances and then take pride in my success, but my mission in life may not be what is best for me. In moving forward I take the position of leader but my mission, given by my wise commander, is to "be still". Lonely at times, and sometimes in the silence life may seem to be passing me by unnoticed, but His voice is heard saying "I am in control and all things will work together for your good"(Romans 8:28). Creator with power is my captain, and in His hands I am secure and will have victory, but I must trust in stillness that victory is in my God, not in myself.

Be Still

The enemy wins when I forge ahead
He lays the traps and snares I dread
Trusting myself to find my way
Has proven my feet are made of clay
I stumble and falter as life is unsure
The future unknown, I'm so insecure
But God, the omniscient, sees the path that is right
He can see to the end and the war I must fight
His command is "Be still, I know the plan
I am your Captain, I have been very man
In suffering, the war I have already won
Remember my battle the work has been done"
The plan for my life is triumph in calm
The stillness I find when I rest in God's palm
In His hands I am held, secure and blessed
My God assures me in Him I can rest

Tyrone Brown

"He is not here, for he is risen, as he said. Come, see the place where the Lord lay." Matthew 28:6

Perhaps one of the greatest verses we can contemplate on is, "He is not here, for he is risen, as he said. Come, see the place where the Lord lay." (Matthew 28:6), as our salvation rests on this fact. There would be no saviour if He was still in the tomb. As Peter and John looked in, the grave clothes and head napkin were empty, and spices were the fragrance left behind. After Lazarus was in the grave, it was said that his body would stink from decay. The Lord's body never decayed and death never laid hold of Him. As lasting immortality is who He is, it was impossible that His body would give way to corruption. Peter was amazed at what he saw, but John believed it was real resurrection. Real faith is what our Lord desires, as He said to Thomas "Blessed are they who have not seen yet have believed" (John 20:29). As we look into the garden tomb, are we like John or Peter? As Mary pondered the empty tomb our Lord appeared with His resurrected body as verification of the angel's words, and in love to a woman who had wiped his feet with her tears. Her worship was recognized by our Lord as He appeared to her first. We are awed, but more than that we are worshippers of a risen, glorified Saviour, who gave Himself that we should have His life in us.

Lyndon Brown

...that the living may know that the most High ruleth in the kingdom of men, and giveth it to whomsoever he will, and setteth up over it the basest of men. Daniel 4:17

The author of the greatest book ever written gave us the answer in who governs in our country, whether Canada, United States or any other country in this world. World politics are not controlled through our votes, or by dictators, or king's decrees, but by the supreme Ruler, the God of Heaven. There is tremendous uncertainty in our global political affairs, with economic concerns and religious beliefs causing divisions and wars. Past history provides us with wars, persecution, utter tyranny and hate, which would hardly seem to show supreme control, but the pitfalls of the human race have a price in death and destruction. The avenger of the souls of men is still the god of this world, and our Lord has allowed him to terrorize kingdoms and nations, but all within the divine plan.

Pointing to a future day when the Prince of Peace will take the throne as King of kings, we know the bringer of righteous justice and true peace will reign with holiness forever and ever. There will be peace on earth when Christ reigns. "Great power and glory" is the term in scripture, and the wonder is that his Church will reign with him. The politics of earth are in God's plans with future events in mind. We should rest in His choices for our countries and pray for those He puts in power.

Tyrone Brown

"I am the light of the world: he that followeth me shall not walk in darkness, but shall have the light of life." John 8:12

Morning always brings light and a new day. This is a natural occurrence which is a beautiful picture of our Saviour, who brings light and a new day to those who are in darkness. The "brightness of His glory" (Hebrews 1:3) is the expression of His very essence, which is light. Regardless of the darkness which sin has brought to this world, God's brightest declaration of Himself was in the person of our Lord Jesus Christ. This illuminating one has brought life and light to the darkness of a world cursed by sin. His incarnation provided a vessel through which this righteous glory could shine into the night of separation from our God. Teaching His disciples the change that comes through faith in Him, we are given hope and a glimpse into the eternal day which awaits us in His presence forever. With natural light there can be dimness because of clouds, but the light of life never dims or fades as His very being is permanent and perpetual. Though this one is light, He endured the darkness at the cross with holy wrath against sin laid on Him. Thus forgiveness was provided and the true light can now shine on us and through us. Resurrection fulfilled the theme of continuance of His abiding light and the essence of his person as the "light of life".

Light of Life

My walk illuminated by Heaven's light
Through Christ the Lord I now have sight
My blind eyes opened to follow Him
His light dispels the darkness of sin
Glory His by righteous claim
Giving Him His blessed name
Light of life; the eternal sun
As glory shines, from this blessed one
Though human body clothed our Lord
His light shone out through every word
Shining light, His power and grace
Is seen alone in Jesus' face

Tyrone Brown

I can do all things through Christ who strengtheneth me. Phillipians 4:13

Personal experience has proven that my Lord daily pours His strength into me. Despite my failures and short comings with caving into negative thinking, the Lord is always there when I turn to him for help. Power over my insecurity and debilitating anxieties is only found in the Spirit of God, who is victorious over the weakness which drags me down. Working to strengthen my feeble knees, his staff of comfort is there to fully lean on. In all of life's trials, and without strength of my own, the Lord draws alongside and provides hope with assurance, that I'm not alone.

Strength is found in hope and trust
Faith alone in Christ a must
Constant His strength, poured into my soul
Through His Spirit, my cup is full
Calling on Him, He answers my prayer
When I feel weak I know He is there
In positive hope His promise to me
Stand fast in the truth and then you'll be free
Free from worry and life's onerous cares
These burdens I carry I know He shares
This unlimited strength is ever present in me
Peace then endures, giving hope endlessly

Tyrone Brown

Now faith is the substance of things hoped for, the evidence of things not seen. Hebrews 11:1

Perhaps faith is one of the most foreign concepts to many in our world today, but it is a reality to every believer in the Lord Jesus Christ. The promise of faith is eternal hope with blessing. Some may doubt the existence of God, and evidence is considered to be non-existent, but the creation around us is impossible without a creator. Within the heart of every individual is a God consciousness with a responsibility to believe that God is. Personal belief is a choice, as in the scriptures faith is the requirement for salvation. There is understanding of the triune God through the creation and this is the first building block of faith.

Without doubt, there is evidence God loves the world, in the person of the Lord Jesus Christ, in His death, burial and resurrection as our saviour. It is personal faith in Him which gives us the promised blessing of eternal life, which is our assured hope. The Word of God reveals His mind and will, which is absolute truth, and therefore can be relied upon completely. With total confidence we know eternal life in Heaven is our sure hope, without contradiction. We are personally going to look on the nail prints of our Saviour and reign with Him eternally.

God's attribute is truth indeed
Approach to Him is faith we need
Omnipotent Word spoke the world into place
The sun and the moon and the stars up in space
The evidence, as plain as light
By faith revealed a hope so bright
We know assurance through God's own word
Placing our trust in our risen Lord
Our universe is proof He is
But greater still I know I'm His
He gave His Son to prove His love
Hope now is resting in Christ above

Lyndon Brown

...God was in Christ reconciling the world unto himself ... II Corinthians 5:19

My wonder in the fact that "God was in Christ" will never cease. It permeates my thoughts when I consider the person of the Lord Jesus Christ. Knowing who He was here on earth, He is not only "Jesus", but he is the "Lord Jesus Christ". Putting emphasis on Lord and Christ (Acts 2:36) elevates Him to deity beyond His humanity. It defines Him as "my God", when His full title is used. Rather often He is referred to as "Jesus", not with completeness of who He really is. When we title Him we worship Him in His supreme place as Lord and King, as well as Saviour. Looking beyond this world into eternity, lasting honour and glory will be to Christ, and every knee will bow confessing Him Lord (Phillipians 2:10, 11). Spiritual power and glory are His right and we should solemnly consider this when we worship Him.

Tyrone Brown

Fight the good fight of faith, lay hold on eternal life. I Timothy 6:12

Wherefore take unto you the whole armour of God, that ye may be able to withstand in the evil day, and having done all to stand. Stand therefore, having your loins girt about with truth, and having on the breastplate of righteousness; And your feet shod with the preparation of the gospel of peace; Above all, taking the shield of faith, wherewith ye shall be able to quench all the fiery darts of the wicked. And take the helmet of salvation, and the sword of the Spirit, which is the word of God. Ephesians 6:13 - 17

We war spiritually every day, but we have the victory in our Lord Jesus Christ. Every move we make, as a Christian, is being challenged by Satan and his adversaries and our battle is fought only through the power of prayer and God's word. With His righteousness, the spiritual breastplate guards our heart with love for Him and our fellow believers. The shoes of the gospel of peace will take that message of love, we know experientially, to those who know suffering and sin. Personal conviction will have its way through God's word which is a two edged sword. Salvation is our helmet protecting our minds from continual bombardment of evil thoughts, doubts and questionings. Our Lord provides us with the armour and the weapons but faith must put it on and use God's word to win the fight. The hope of eternal life is the prize, so we must never lose sight of the final reward of Heaven with Christ in glory.

Tyrone Brown

In everything give thanks: for this is the will of God in Christ Jesus concerning you. I Thessalonians 5:1

Regardless of our circumstances, it is the eternal word and will of God that we give thanks. As personal trials form thoughts of "Why me?", and anxiety takes control, the one who knows our every inward thought says "Oh give thanks unto the Lord for he is good" (Psalm136:1). We overcome with thanksgiving as we replace our negative thoughts with positive, and occupy our mind with our blessings. Inward occupation with worship and thanksgiving of our Saviour will empower the Christian to put life's concerns, pain and sorrow in perspective, in light of eternity. Our problems are known by the one who talked to the leper and commended him for returning to give thanks, and blessed him for it. There is blessing in thanksgiving, as it focuses our eyes on the one from whom all blessings flow. It is the will of God that we look for something to be thankful for in every situation of life, with positive thoughts overcoming the trial that would bring us down. The greatest thing we can be thankful for is our Saviour and the gift of salvation. God's plan is that we would be "to the praise of His glory" (Ephesians 1:12), and thanksgiving for the gift of His Son is the outward demonstration of this. Thankfulness should mark every Christian, and a positive attitude with peace and joy will be the result. "Thanks be unto God for his unspeakable gift." II Corinthians 9:15.

Only thanksgiving gives peace to my mind
The power to remove thoughts of the negative kind
Reproof to "poor me" and questions of "Why ?"
Reasonings that hurt and cause me to cry
Thankfulness turns despair to bright hope
Puts all in perspective so in life I can cope
In thanksgiving I turn my eyes to the One
Who gave His life and God's work has done
His unspeakable gift causes praise to His name
Glory to Him who is always the same
Regardless the pain or suffering I feel
Thanksgiving will bring a joy that will heal

Lyndon Brown

I will instruct thee and teach thee in the way which thou shalt go: I will guide thee with mine eye. Psalm 32:8

Irrespective of my circumstances or my challenges, the mighty God, who is my Father, has promised he will guide me with unswerving wisdom and love, the way my life should take. Greater presence than the most powerful men of earth, and greater wisdom than the most educated men of institutes of learning, is the promise to His child. Leading with His all-seeing eye is the one who knows the end from the beginning, guiding through the valleys and over the mountain tops, under the dark storms of threatening fear and in the bright sunshine of joy and peace, in the lonely path of hurt and in the happy halls of comfort, with omniscient intelligence. The hope a believer has is founded in the omniscience of an omnipotent God, who is omnipresent with His thoughts and love for His own. Peace is ours when we commit our ways to our Saviour, who has promised to never leave us nor forsake us (Hebrews 13:5), and has promised to guide us with His eye. Putting our trust in Him, our instruction is given through his word, for He is the Word. There is no greater teacher than the Spirit of God, or higher place of learning than in the knowledge written in the inspired Word of God. Life often can seem uncertain and circumstances difficult to understand, but we must be content in knowing, beyond a shadow of doubt, he is guiding with his eye.

Peace through trust in my Lord and friend
He knows my ways from beginning to end
Omniscient God who knows what is right
Providing His guidance with Heaven's Light
The omnipotent God understands my need
His Spirit within my soul will lead
Power divine will answer prayer
His promise is given that He does care
Omnipresent God gives strength for each day
Teaching truth with grace, along life's way
His eye is watching me from above
Guiding my path with a Father's love

Tyrone Brown

No man hath seen God at any time. If we love one another God dwelleth in us and his love is perfected in us. I John 4:12

You and I are the place where God dwells only. It is our privilege and responsibility to let His love be manifested in us and through us. In my life, present at all times, is the Spirit of God as comforter and my new nature. There must be portrayed in me Christ likeness and the love of God. The thought that God is revealed to the world through us is the greatest wonder and privilege there is. Living each day, the love of God gives infinite pleasure to us as believers, but also tremendous responsibility to our God and Father. How fortunate that we are blessed with the indwelling Holy Spirit, as we have no power of our own to be like our Lord and Saviour. The love of God is living and real, as a continuing flow. It is not an act of love but a continuing outpouring of the very essence of love "for God is love" (I John 4:8). Chosen to be His vessel and messenger is the astounding truth we are given in this verse. Living out this truth must be our daily goal and priority.

How can I portray the love of God? First and foremost we are told to love one another. I John is very clear that our love for one another is evidence that God dwells in us. It is your and my love that perfects His love here on earth. When we care in ways like an encouraging word, showing empathy for a fellow believer going through a trial, sympathy for the one who mourns, understanding for the one who struggles socially or emotionally, or what addresses the needs of another, is His love shining out through us. When we offer a smile to strangers, or kindness to someone who is homeless, we are commending our God and the Lord Jesus Christ, not ourselves. Reading our actions is the world that does not know the Saviour we worship. The mission we are sent on is divine, and of utmost importance as the God of Heaven would have us perfect His love.

The love of God outshines through me
It is so wondrous that I should be
The instrument of His own choice
My life, reflection of His voice
In power of the Spirit's love
My life portrays my God above
The dwelling of His love and grace
The radiance of Christ's lovely face
Is in my heart to shine His light
Into a world that's found in night
Oh may His love be perfected in me
Continually flowing to others, freely

Tyrone Brown

Thanks be unto God who giveth us the victory through our Lord Jesus Christ. I Corinthians 15: 37

Times of battle are in every believer's life and in the fight and struggle the "Captain of our salvation" champions the way to victory, as He has gone through this before and won a victory which no other could ever win. His triumph has validated His leadership, and His willingness to go into the battle for us verifies His love. When our Lord Jesus Christ fought the darkness of sin's hold, the completeness of His work was stated in His word "Finished". The resurrection was the evidence of God's satisfaction in the deliverance from sin's curse, which had bound the human race from the fall in the Garden of Eden. Through His accomplishment we have the reality of continual strength and power over the battle against the world, the flesh and the devil. The Holy Spirit, who indwells us, gives the focus we need, which is the person of Christ, who will lead us to victory. (For if God be for us, who can be against us. Romans 8:31) We have the victory already but we must avail ourselves of the power which the triune God has promised to all who believe.

Victory

Great is our Captain, triumphant in war
He won the battle when our sins He bore
With triumph He rose with God's power over death
Witness to the claim He gave man the first breath
This leader in spiritual warfare ascended on high
With His conquest completed, we never will die
As our defender, He gives power to fight
The powers of darkness which hinder the light
Giving deliverance, the victory is ours
His promise which keeps us through trials dark hours
The battle is over, for the faith we contend
The crown of righteousness for His glory, our end

Tyrone Brown

I am the resurrection and the life: he that believeth in me, though he were dead, yet shall he live. John 11:25

The promise of fondant coloured eggs and chocolate bunnies is how many think of Easter. Our pretty decorations of purple, pink and yellow flowered baskets and sweet lemon coloured chicks gives the holiday a pleasant feeling and light hearted air. Is this the true meaning of Easter? We have a far greater event that should cause us to celebrate and rejoice. There was once the darkest hours in our world's history, on the Good Friday we now celebrate. It was the day our Saviour was crucified. Powers of darkness were given time to unleash their hatred with vengeance against the Lord of Heaven and earth. The suffering of the Lord Jesus Christ at the hands of men was extreme and insufferable, and as unethical as this world has ever seen. But, these sufferings pale in comparison to the anguish He felt when the judgement of God for sin was poured out on Him "who did no sin" (I Peter 2:22), and "in whom was no sin" (I John 3:5). His cry at the end of these darkest hours "Finished!" is what our souls can rest in for a completed salvation. This world that crucified the Lord of life and glory was the world He came to save. However, His death alone would not be enough if God had not raised Him from the dead. The victory of resurrection is the true meaning of Easter. The triumph over death and the grave is why we can truly live with new life in Him. Choosing to give the Lord Jesus Christ the place of honour and worship is what we should do when we consider the great salvation He provided through His death, burial and resurrection(I Corinthians 15:1-4)

Hatred, scorn, rejection, pain
The Lamb of God for me was slain
Having come to save the lost
Christ has paid the awful cost
His word resounds with power and might
"Finished" my Lord has won the fight
The greatest battle ever fought
Was when God's son salvation brought
Power over death, He rose victorious
His tomb is empty, the truth how glorious
Resurrection divine; eternal He stands
Points to the wounds in His side and His hands
His victory unmatched; His love without bounds
Forever in Heaven His name will resound

Tyrone Brown

O Lord, how manifold are thy works! In wisdom thou hast made them all: the earth is full of thy riches. Psalm 104:24

To the world of atheists, this beautiful creation of God's hand is just an accident. How sad to never see the wisdom and wonder of our God in creating a universe that is intertwined and balanced. Preserving our tiny earth for His pleasure and presence, He created the earth with everything necessary for life. The wonders of our planet can only stem from an omniscient and omnipotent God who planned it and formed it. Probability aside, you and I have within us a God consciousness which cannot be denied, though many try to prove He does not exist. There is no greater lie than the one we are taught in our schools, that this universe we are living in is only by chance and not a creation of God.

The wonder of creation causes us to consider the one who designed it, and His purpose in our being. We read He created us in His image (Genesis 1:27) and desired to have fellowship with us, but the fall of Adam brought an end to this relationship. The greater wonder now is the wisdom and love of God in providing salvation. When wonder becomes worship we fulfill the plan of God from eternity past ("that we should be to the praise of his glory" (Ephesians 1:12)). Returning praise to the one who "upholds all things by the word of his power" (Hebrews 1:3), who was the Word who came to be our Saviour, and is the risen glorified Saviour in Heaven, is the purpose for which we were made, and there is blessing in worship. The riches of our God are seen in creation and the riches of His grace are seen in our Saviour, the Lord Jesus Christ.

We cannot fathom God's power and might
Beyond our thought His creation of light
He spoke the word and it was done
Declared the moon, the stars, the sun
Never before a flower had grown
Never a corn of wheat was sown
He had a plan; His voice was heard
The rivers flowed just by His word
He made the plants that had the seed
He knew what growing plants would need
Skies of blue He designed for flight
Creating the eagle with amazing sight
The fish He created to swim in the sea
With colours that reflect His unrivaled beauty
The trail of His work in order it stood
The animals He made and saw it was good
In this marvelous world He created a man
With His breath of life He completed the plan
Power and might His creation portrays
Wisdom and strength in His work He displays

Lyndon Brown

Which hope we have as an anchor of the soul, both sure and steadfast Hebrews 6:19

Prone to drift we are like ships which need an anchor in a harbour of safety. In assurance that we have an anchor that is both sure and steadfast, we live with an eternal hope which is perpetually the security that we are the redeemed children of God. There may be storms in our life with winds of adversity but our Saviour is entered into our haven of rest and secured our eternal salvation. There is no greater anchor than the eternal Son of God. With the inseparable link to the anchor we will not drift or run aground with fear of sinking, but are tethered to the one who is entered into Heaven. This presents us with the responsibility to chart our course in accordance to the Word of God, preserving our ship and giving us the blessed hope that is before us.

Where is there safety in a storm at sea? Anchored in a harbour is the evident answer. Having had a life of storms and tempest with disability and anxiety my confidence is in the Anchor of my soul. The hope I have in my Lord and Saviour keeps me secure, regardless how fierce the winds of adversity blow. His promise is that the hope He has begun will be completed when He brings me into Heaven's rest. Perhaps life takes us through calm waters at times, but storms are essential to appreciate the anchor and harbour of safety found in Christ alone.

Hope perfected, complete one day
My anchor secure in Christ, the Way
Tethered to the one who does not move
Through storms of life His presence prove
Though fierce winds blow, my ship's secure
Divine deliverer, whose love will endure
Forever He's entered my haven of rest
My anchor of hope, how great and how blessed

Tyrone Brown

But the fruit of the Spirit is love, joy, peace, longsuffering, gentleness, goodness, faith. Galatians 5:22

Having the indwelling Holy Spirit, the life of a believer ought to manifest the life found in the seed within. The fruit produced by a tree indicates the seed which it began from. Creation has given us vivid pictures which we can apply to our Christian life with the help of our Lord. The fruits which He wants us to produce are righteousness and holiness. This translates into the Spirit's fruit we read of in Galatians 5:22. The basis of the fruit is love, and we know that our "God is love"(I John 4:8), so His very character should flow out through us. This source produces His promise that our joy may be full and His promise that His "peace which passeth all understanding will guard our mind through Christ Jesus. (Phillipians 4:7). Through the consideration of love, with joy and peace, the other characteristics become the life fulfilling attributes we should produce. Longsuffering has the nature of our God, as He is "longsuffering not willing that any should perish" (II Peter 3:9). We have the responsibility to have constant trust that in our Christian life we are working out the purposes and plan of God and never lose sight of the confirmation that awaits us, "Well done my good and faithful servant". The gentleness we witnessed in our Lord Jesus, as He fed the multitudes and spoke to the children, is our greatest example of the fruit He desires us to produce. The Spirit, through the believer, is giving the world the blessing of our Saviour's person with gentleness, goodness, meekness and self control. His work through you and me is to provide the perishing a witness to the blessings which God has for all those who have faith in Him. Salvation through faith is the beginning, or germinating of the seed, but daily faith and trust is the continuance of growth with God's sheltering care.

God planted the seeds within my soul
Planted within for the Spirit's role
To harvest fruit with His glory so sweet
The fruits we live to lay at His feet
When love was planted life changed within
From weeds and thorns sown all through sin
To fruits of joy and lasting peace
Long suffering, gentleness, with much increase
Patience and meekness He harvests with grace
Fruit reflecting the love of Christ's face

Tyrone Brown

those things which are before, I press toward the mark for the prize of the high calling of God in Christ Jesus. Phillipians 3:13-14

In life there will be memories producing personal desires to go back to live in the past. These times when we felt safe and successful, with happiness and joy, but life is not stagnant but constantly changing. What the Christian knows is that though life changes, our God never changes and His promise is "I will never, never leave you nor forsake you." (Hebrews 13:5) With His much needed presence and guidance we must take change in life, as a course changes for a long distance runner, and continue with perseverance the race before us. Hope for a first place finish is always the goal of an athlete, and the believer's goal is the greatest hope centered on Christ Jesus, with the commendation of God our father. The calling has considerable significance as we reach forward for distinction from the greatest Majesty in Heaven. Who can please himself with contentment to finish the race somewhere in the middle of the contestants? The race is both competitive and difficult, but the prize is more glorious than the commendation of the world, when our life is merely taken up with success in the things of this life. We must reach forward, without looking back, for the finish line is the goal with Christ's commendation "Well done". We started well; now let us continue with the hope going forward, conscious that our Lord will crown us when we reach our Heavenly goal.

Not what is past but what is ahead
Life is not stagnant but a challenge instead
The race is not run by the one without heart
It only is won, seeing the goal from the start
Not the prize of worldly gain
Not success of wealth and fame
The goal is the One who has run on before
He secured the prize when my sins He bore
The high calling of God is the goal of the race
The prize to win, to look on Christ's face

Tyrone Brown

Christ is all and in all. Colossians 3:11

There is contempt by the world of the Saviour, who is God's complete answer to every aspect of life. This Christ is beyond our finite minds to grasp, yet there are some who would seek to express Him as a prophet or a good person in history. This limitation of His person is an insult to Almighty God, as He portrayed more than goodness; He was the complete revelation of God in human form. There is none greater or pre-eminent to our Lord Jesus Christ, and He fills all positions of authority and power. Reserved for Him alone, is Heaven's worship and song.

When I consider His majesty and greatness, I am humbled at the fact that I am His very own purchased possession, child and friend. He cares in love about my every need, and continually helps me along life's journey. Finding provision for a daily walk there is strength, and having His strength there is power to overcome the trials that threaten to pull me down. His unequalled joy and peace free me from the fetters of self and unhappy thoughts, which bring anxiety and fear. With the continuous presence of the one who "is all and in all", the assurance of God's best for my life is a reality and Heaven is my living hope.

Tyrone Brown

Blessed is the man that walketh not in the counsel of the ungodly, nor standeth in the way of sinners, nor sitteth in the seat of the scornful. But his delight is in the law of the Lord and in his law doth he meditate day and night. Psalm 1:1-2

Wisdom requires the control that comes from fellowship with the God who created us for His companion. The first man, Adam, walked with God with wisdom and understanding. When given counsel by Satan, who is the founder of ungodliness, eternal destruction and misery were the result. Destroying the pleasure and blessing we have when we are in fellowship with our Lord, walking with ones who have made light of the salvation through our Lord Jesus Christ, we lose out in life. When we walk with unbelievers we give place to their ways and soon we are found standing outside of both worship and service for our Saviour. There is no room for the Word of God that condemns the sinner and his ways. Standing eventually leads to sitting, and we become comfortable with hearing our God's name taken in vain and the ridicule of the laws of our God.

However, the Spirit of God indwells us and blesses our life when we walk in daily fellowship with our Lord. We are led with wisdom and power to conquer the insidious ways of ungodliness which would take hold of us and lead us down the wrong path. The Word of God is where we find the source of the power to overcome the world. Enjoying the salvation which is ours, will keep us from desiring the places where the world finds its fleeting enjoyment. Though free from the power of sin, having the Spirit of God indwelling us, the flesh can still draw our thoughts and lives away from the Word of God and fellowship with our Lord. We have hope with joy as we walk together as friends and chosen disciples of our Lord Jesus Christ. The blessing of the Christian is a promise which God, who cannot lie, has given and we can stand upon His word. We walk with purpose, we stand with promise, and we sit with His presence, when we come before Him in worship. What soul is not affected with calmness and peace when sitting still with the knowledge that God is choosing to guide, with assurance, the child he has delivered from the ungodly?

Tyrone Brown

Cast not away your confidence which hath great recompense of reward. Hebrews 10:35

Creating trust, one must be genuine and faithful to his promise. Our saviour has proven Himself worthy of our complete trust, and we know, as God, He cannot lie and so His promises are "yea and in Him amen" (II Corinthians 1:20). There is hope in every trial and difficult circumstance of life that we encounter and confidence that our Lord will hear our heart's prayer to give us strength to overcome the adversity. Trust often falters and faith becomes weak, but God never changes and He never leaves us. Confidence establishes great reward as the giver has been shown trustworthy in providing salvation through His death on the cross.

The patient waiting for the return of our Lord is preparing us for the Heavenly commendation "Well done, good and faithful servant". History often affects the world's thinking that since our Lord hasn't fulfilled His promise of returning He isn't going to come, but we know without hesitation that He will come, returning to govern, but we will be with Him as His heirs. Having His promise should strengthen our resolve to be patient in all life's situations and trials, living to bring glory to Him. The written promise is "great reward".

My heart in patience waits His return
Eternal blessing, the reward to earn
There awaits my Saviour on His glorified throne
His the worship, and His alone
With confidence I wait, knowing the truth is sure
With hope in His Word, that is steadfast and pure
Patience in trials is also my goal
Knowing with confidence, He's in control
Experience would teach I have hope in my Lord
The promise He gives, I'll have "great reward"

Tyrone Brown

And this is life eternal, that they might know thee the only true God, and Jesus Christ, whom thou hast sent. John 17:3

Reasoning has often deterred man from having truth revealed through the very one who is truth. Having faith requires us to accept, unconditionally, what the Word of God teaches and reveals about the true God and the Lord Jesus Christ. Life gives man responsibility because it began by the breath of God's mouth, and He designed us to live eternally. However, sin has interrupted what our God intended for the human race. The desire of the Lord Jesus Christ, in His prayer to His Father, just before he went to the cross, was that we would know this eternal life and the greatest gift we were ever given. The issue we must come to face is our sin before a holy God, and the responsibility we have is to repent and turn to the true God and Jesus Christ. His life then is promised, with not only the hope of being eternal but also of being abundant (John 10:10), with joy (John 17:13) and peace (John 14:27). Personal faith means a personal knowledge of God himself, which is revealed in Jesus Christ. It is beyond our minds to grasp that the God of Heaven delivered His Son for children of disobedience, that as children we might be heirs with Christ (Romans 8:17) and enjoy the life of God eternally. (Ephesians 2:7 That in the ages to come he might show the exceeding riches of his grace in his kindness toward us through Christ Jesus.)

The God of truth we want to know
His Son, the Christ, His life did show
Eternal the Word, eternal the Son
Infinite love in the work that was done
Though He died in our stead, sin's curse He bore
The power of death unlocked evermore
Through Jesus my Saviour not only I live
But His peace and joy He's promised to give
Daily I learn God's life, joy and peace
Life that has given sin's captive release
Eternal life in knowing His grace
Forever I'll worship when I look on His face

Tyrone Brown

And to know the love of Christ, which passeth knowledge...Ephesians 3:19

Though the heart may be weak in its human capacity to love without wavering, the love of Christ is eternal and steadfast. Personal appreciation of this divine love can only come through the Holy Spirit's revelation to a believer's heart. We have known the love of God in the giving of His Son, to provide salvation through the sacrifice for sin at the cross of Calvary. In acceptance of His gift we have experienced His love in forgiveness of our sins and in the adoption of sons (Galatians 4:5) having now become a child of God. Prior to the fulfillment of the plan of salvation, our Lord prayed that we would know His love within our souls (John 17:26). Producing the love within us is the work of the Holy Spirit,but we must be occupied with the reading of the word of God and with prayer.

When we consider love we think about the characteristics it presents, such as kindness, compassion, care, devotion and faithfulness, but the love of Christ is far beyond this as He is "love"(I John 4:8). The very essence of His being is unequivocal love. The comparison of our human love to divine love is poultry, at best. Pure love, with the ability to reach from the holiest in Heaven to the darkness of a sin cursed earth, is more than our finite minds can comprehend. Chosen in Christ before the foundation of the world (Ephesians 1:4) is both incredible and immeasurable, conveying divine love which we will never fully understand. However, the exhortation is that we should continually focus our minds on Christ, that we would know His love in experience daily, so that through worship we will know His presence and joy.

Love beyond all human thought
Love that God's salvation brought
Love that is pure, steadfast and true
Love that has reached down to me and to you
Love that my heart knows everyday
Love that has promised to guide my way
Love in perfection that stood in my place
Love that is seen in Christ's beautiful face
Love in the person of God's blessed Son
Love is the essence of the Holy One
Love that passes the knowledge of man
Love that devised salvation's plan

Tyrone Brown

And we know that all things work together for good to them that love God, to them who are called according to His purpose. Romans 8:28

The foundation which our lives are built upon is God, who created all things. It is absolute and unmoveable. His loving kindness has designed the purpose in the details of our individual lives. Our circumstances are not by chance, but are the deliberate plan of one who is omniscient and omnipotent. In His plan there is need for construction with strength, combined with a purpose. My life is not a facade which gives an impression with no use, but is the house of the Spirit of God, proving His presence in personal fulfillment. I am constrained to live life as my Lord, as a living sacrifice (Romans 12:1), committed to His plan. The power to live out this plan is found in God's indwelling Holy Spirit, bringing the satisfaction that life has a purpose. The wonderful blessing is that the building will have His approval, fulfilling the promise that "all things will work together for good".

Unfailing is our Lord's design
Though fear and doubt may fill my mind
With promise for my good He moves
Throughout my life as He must choose
The plan, both soul and body takes
Directs my path with no mistakes
Loving care His power displays
As He guides through difficult ways
His promise is sure, it will not fail
Hope holds the key, as the plan He'll unveil

Tyrone Brown

For we have not an high priest which cannot be touched with the feeling of our infirmities; but was in all points tempted (tested) like as we are, yet without sin Hebrews 4:15

The eternal will of God was manifest in His Son, in the fulfilment of the once and for all sacrifice for sin. His acceptance of the sacrifice is grounded in the resurrection of our Lord Jesus Christ from the dead. As both my sacrifice and priest, He intercedes for me before God, utterly accepted because of His perfection in His condescension as a man. Holiness has found its meaning in the person of our Lord Jesus Christ, and this reveals God's requirement of a high priest. Without sin, because He could not sin, as He never ceased to be God, His righteous claim as our Great High Priest is absolute and unchangeable. His position is without question, cancelling the old order of sacrifices brought before God, first for the high priest and then for the sins of the people. With such a High Priest we have boldness to enter into the very presence of God, and now our Father (Hebrews 10:19). His life in humility, loneliness, misunderstanding and pain now fits Him completely to intercede for us, with understanding and compassion. Entering into every trial that we face in life as He experienced the suffering of every feeling of weakness and pain we experience. The difficulties life provides might seem like we are alone in our suffering, but God's holy Son never leaves us or forsakes us (Hebrews 13:5), as He is touched by the feeling of our infirmities. Can we ever comprehend the love of God in providing such a sacrifice and faithful High Priest?

High Priest in perfection God's son came in love
In holiness now stands in God's presence above
His place is eternal; His sacrifice complete
In Heaven He shows pierced hands and pierced feet
Presenting the wounds of Calvary's cross
He suffered for sin with such anguish and loss
His life was given, poured out for me
God's claims were met, so I am now free
With passionate love, written now on His heart
My High Priest knows my pains from the start
Touched by my feelings, with having been here
He knows my trials, difficulties and tears
My faithful High Priest in love intercedes
With righteous forgiveness to His Father he pleads

Tyrone Brown

He shall see of the travail of His soul, and shall be satisfied Isaiah 53:11

Can we comprehend God's satisfaction in the completion of salvation's plan? Pause for a moment to contemplate the Saviour's words "It is finished!". His words were the fulfillment of this prophecy that the Father would be fully satisfied with His suffering for sin, when He bore the wrath of God against our rebellion and disobedience. Hundreds of years before our Lord came, words were given to the prophet Isaiah that the completed work of our Lord Jesus Christ would satisfy the righteous claims of holy God, once and for all. How do we know God was satisfied? The third day the resurrection heralded the approval of the Father, when he raised Him from the dead. The Saviour was also satisfied, as He came forth in power of His own accord. From death to life - the divine stamp of approval that salvation was seen as complete and verified. We have the assurance that we can rest completely in salvation, provided at infinite cost by our Lord Jesus Christ. If God is satisfied what can I add to it? Perfect in Christ I stand and all I can do is worship Him.

Plan of the ages God's hope in the Son
Hope for a world that was lost and undone
Outshining God's goodness, and the truth of His grace
The perfection of godliness seen in His face
The Son of the Father was all His delight
Fulfilling salvation in the darkest of night
"Finished" was heard, the work was complete
The work that was done will never repeat
Resurrected in power, the Father was pleased
Satisfied with the sacrifice, His work on earth ceased

Tyrone Brown

Fear thou not; for I am with thee: be not dismayed; for I am thy God: I will strengthen thee; yea, I will help thee; yea, I will uphold thee with the right hand of my righteousness. Isaiah 41:10

The presence of our Lord is never in doubt, continual and abiding, never ceasing and absolute. It is a promise which is true and sure; never shaken or put to question. As it is the word of the one who is Yea and Amen. Yes we falter and have hindrances in our lives, but His word is "I will never leave you or forsake you". Pondering who God is we realize the power of His presence to dispel fear and anxiety. Hope and trust in our God and eternal Saviour delivers us from fear and the negative thoughts which bind us. His promise continues with strength and upholding power. The divine strength is the greatest builder of confidence that will hold us up through trials, regardless of our weakness. Faith is a must if we are to overcome with the power that is from the one who sits on the throne of Heaven. What a privilege to have the God of the universe right by my side, strengthening and upholding me.

More than a guardian watching over me
Provider of strength, and my surety
God of the universe; friend by my side
Promises never to leave, but with me He'll abide
In confident trust my life in His hand
Born of His Spirit, dependant man here I stand
Heaven's righteousness holds me with power divine
What a wonder to lean on this Saviour of mine

Tyrone Brown

Blessed is the man whose strength is in thee Psalm 84:5

Life has many obstacles in its way and hills to climb, which challenge us and require an inner strength to overcome. Reaching goals and fighting battles is not for the faint of heart but is as much a part of life as the air we breathe. So where does inner strength come from? As a believer in the Lord Jesus Christ, my strength alone is from His Spirit, who lives in me. Each time I stumble He lifts me up; each time I feel weary He comes alongside; and when I feel lonely He whispers "I will never leave you or forsake you." Without the strength of my Lord I am weak and so feeble. Having a disabled body has meant my struggles have been many, but power to overcome the fiercest battle of psychological anxieties and feelings of worthlessness have come from the promises written in the Word of God. The strength He gives is not false happiness but true strength to face the struggles and trials. Real, true, peace and joy, no matter the circumstances of life. Who has power over death? The same Lord who walks with me every step that I take, so the power to keep me will never fail. Truly I am blessed.

Lyndon Brown

Poetry from the Heart

Big Changes Someday

God will make us perfect someday
Happy, so happy, we'll be perfect someday
The nearer to Heaven the triumph is sure
Great thought this will happen
He's promised it's true
Hope is so blessed the heart longs to see
The change to be like Him and perfect someday

Few will be asking the saints in that day
What were your trials and cause of dismay
The song in that day will be gladness and joy
Our Lord to behold Him
His likeness to wear
Dress us in glory forever to share
To be like Him, with Him and perfect someday

Tyrone Brown

The One Who Is

Before the Savior was born on that night
The inn had no room for this one who is Light
The shepherds heard the hosts above
Sing "Glory to God" for the one who is Love
The wisemen came from the east to bring
Gifts to the one who is our King
His parents fled to Egypt to stay
For Herod would kill the one who is the Way
Baptized in Jordan the Father was heard
"This is my beloved son", the one who is the Word
Going with purpose to Galilee's shore
Teaching the multitude, the one who is the Door
They crucified Him in mockery and strife
But He is risen, the one who is Life
In wonder we ponder the life of the Lamb
Jesus our savior who is the great "I am"
Now with this Saviour at the door of your heart
Will you open to Him, His grace He'll impart

Tyrone Brown

The Heavenly Child

Bethlehem cradled the Heavenly child
The one who was meek, lowly and mild
Incarnate God, He came to earth
Perfect and holy at His birth
Heralding His presence, the angels sang
"Glory to God" through the heavens rang
This miracle had, hope clothed as man
He came as God's salvation plan
Deliverer from sin's curse that bound
The greatest gift in Him is found
Great gift of life and boundless love
God's son was sent from Heaven above
Now being blessed sing out His praise
Hallelujahs with thanksgiving raise

Tyrone Brown

Both Lord and Christ

More than humanity; reason to ponder
Person of Godhead, ever I wonder
Eternally the Son, true image of God
In perfection He lived as His feet this earth trod
Returning to Heaven He was given a name
The title His right, He is ever the same
Lord of lords, His power and might
With love the Savior won the fight
As King, He sits on God's right hand
Our eternal destiny in His command
To Him all must bow; this exalted one
In worship I bow to God's righteous Son
"Lord Jesus Christ" this name He was given
Ever the same, forever in Heaven

Tyrone Brown

Can We Hope that Morning Breaks

Can we hope that morning breaks?
Has Heaven's sunrise as we awake?
The darkness of our trials passed
The night seen hopeless gone at last
In God's time our lessons He teaches
The hand of our Saviour to us He outreaches
With purpose His children He brings through the night
Guiding our way with Heavenly light
The reason we may not understand
Though we know it is the way He planned
Hard the road and rough the way
But dawn will bring the light of day
When His purpose He will make known
The determinate council of God will be shown

Tyrone Brown

Comfort

The more God takes His children through
The more we know His word is true
He is with us, great His love
In nearness holds us like a glove
In His hands we are secure
Though through the pain we must endure
The care must now on Him be cast
His promise cannot let pain last
We call on Him to strengthen you
To comfort, help and bring you through

Tyrone Brown

Creation's Truth

Inescapable, God's power to create
With wisdom designing the small and the great
Elephants roaming where dryness abounds
Insects with purpose our mind it astounds
Volcanoes erupting regaining control
Rivers of lava with fire take a toll
But out of the ashes new life will appear
Resurrection in flora, the picture is clear
Particles of dust, to the oceans of fish
Plan of the ages our Creator's grand wish
Amazing the workings of this universe wide
Intelligence of a Creator, the truth we can't hide

Lyndon Brown

He is Risen

The powers of darkness surrounded God's son
Owning the hour as they railed at this One
Binding His hands as He knelt to pray
In Gethsemane's garden, before the break of day
Without struggle, as a lamb He went
This was the reason from Heaven He was sent
They hated Him without a cause
They accused Him then of breaking God's laws
His kingship they mocked with a crown of thorn
And a robe of purple on His back was worn
Furrows they ploughed with the scourge that whipped
His coat without seam from His body was stripped
Outside of the city to Golgotha He was led
The place of a skull, as often it is said
Hands and feet pounded through with nails
As the darkness of judgment against Him assails
God's righteous demands He fulfilled in three hours
With triumph defeated sin's awful power
"It is finished!" He cried then bowed His head
Having dismissed His spirit, they found Him dead
Blood must be shed so a spear pierced His side
With love for lost sinners on the cross He had died
Taking Him down, as a rich man who cared
Buried Him in linen in his tomb which he spared
Fearing His followers would steal Him away
They rolled a large stone to keep the doorway
Three days passed in the shadow of night
Then God rolled back the stone as the tomb filled with light
His linen clothes lay, but no body was found
Resurrected with power, this truth so profound
Ascending to God's right hand now in glory
His redeemed will ever tell out His story
With worship and praise they will sing the great song
Power, glory and strength to Him belong

Lyndon Brown

Home in Heaven

Redeemed by the blood, in His presence is peace
The end of all suffering and there trials cease
There as God's children is our Father of love
Welcoming with grace to His mansion above
The glory of the Saviour fills Heaven with light
Sin gone forever, there'll be no more night
With parting a thing we have known in the past
It has vanished forever; life eternal will last
Crying, tears dried, with no sorrow in Heaven
There is joy in God's presence, all sins are forgiven
The morning will dawn when we meet in the air
The Saviour we'll see; His glory we'll share

Tyrone Brown

Easter

It was the dawn of power over death
No victory had such length or breadth
Only one triumphant claim
Only one with "Life" His name
My Lord with resurrection power
Had triumphed in that terrible hour
"Finished!" He cried, sin's price He had paid
Removing sin's curse, His life He had laid
On the altar at Calvary, in my place He died
Victorious in battle, the truth verified
Raised incorruptible, this one is divine
Saviour and Lord; what a wonder He's mine

Lyndon Brown

The Almighty

His face portrays His character and might
Powerful with wisdom, holiness and light
With authority, He planned the way
This omniscient one our debt would pay
The righteous defender of all that is true
Delivered the lost; sins penalty He knew
With His almighty arm He conquered the foe
Defeated the grave and death here below
Now Great High Priest who knows our needs
Before God our Father He intercedes
In the storms of life His peace He brings
His help and strength, sheltered under His wings
His mighty power is promised to all
Who trust His word and on His name call

Tyrone Brown

Eternal Hope

Believing awards us a hope that's forever
Its foundation is sure; Christ's hold none can sever
Hope that is living, in power over death
Hope in the one who gives our life's breath
Forever he lives and in Him I stand
There securely I'm held in the palm of His hand
Hope that is real; God's word is my trust
Hope that endures, when my bones become dust
This hope rests in Christ, eternal and sure
Rests in His blood, that has made my soul pure

Lyndon Brown

His Guidance

Peace through trust in my Lord and friend
He knows my ways from beginning to end
Omniscient God who knows what is right
Providing His guidance with Heaven's Light
The omnipotent God understands my need
His Spirit within my soul will lead
Power divine will answer prayer
His promise is given that He does care
Omnipresent God gives strength for each day
Teaching truth with grace, along life's way
His eye is watching me from above
Guiding my path with a Father's love

Tyrone Brown

Gethsemane, Gabbatha, Golgotha, the Grave and Glory

As He knelt, the cross on His mind
The agony felt with God's plan for mankind
In Gethsemane's garden God's son knelt to pray
His resolve to die; there was no other way

Pilate was governor at Gabbatha's court
Accused of the people with a false report
With scourge and spitting they ridiculed Him there
Silence His answer to their questions and dare

With the cross on His back He mounted the hill
Golgotha the place reserved in God's will
To suffer for sin, in darkness He cried
Forsaken by God, for my sin there He died

With power over death, the grave had no hold
The stone rolled away; "look in" they were told
The place where He lay, no body was found
Witness to deity, there are no bones in the ground

Through the clouds, in glory He went
The blessed one, God's son who was sent
To Heaven He's gone, my home to prepare
His face I shall see, there is none to compare

Lyndon Brown

Jesus

His light shone in a stable so dark
This "Light of Life" His path would mark
God's peace personified in a small baby boy
His truth has come that we may have joy
The Word made flesh, to dwell with man
Written in prophecy, God's determinate plan
Through power divine He upheld the earth
This little baby to whom Mary gave birth
Son of God; the Creator of all
Prince of Peace, lying in a manger stall
Hope had come for a world bound in sin
Witnessing shepherds His joy found within
"Eternal One"; the "Great I Am"
Possessor of all; God's Son the "Lamb"

Tyrone Brown

Have You Room in Your Heart

Have you room in your heart today
The Savior promises He will come in to stay
With Bethlehem saying "No room in our inn
For Jesus who came to save us from sin"
The world has no room for God's glorious Son
They rejected and scorned the compassionate one
His place on this earth was out in the cold
No bed or soft pillow were His, we are told
Outside of the city on a cross crucified
Alone in the darkness for our sin there He died
Planning to seal Him out of their sight
A stone rolled in place, but God moved it with might
Power over death ever living with grace
His redeemed will bow when they look on His face
Your heart He will enter, you must only believe
Acknowledge your sin and Christ Jesus receive

Lyndon Brown

His Strength

As patiently He takes my hand
Eternal strength is mine to stand
Obeying His word, there is joy in my soul
Power over weakness, which seems to control
This body is feeble but His strength is sure
True to His promise, both constant and pure
He will not falter, though I stumble and fall
Power He gives me to overcome all
The omnipotent God is my saviour and friend
He's walking beside me and will to the end

Lyndon Brown

His Silence

Without a word the Saviour spoke
With silence their conscience He awoke
God's words complete, He would not speak
Though answers Pilate then did seek
His life in perfect truth had been
The purpose of His life been seen
Water of Life and Bread from Heaven
His life for us must then be given
Telling more by silent grief
His accusers stood in unbelief
As witness to His righteous claim
They nailed the one whose very name
Told of salvation for fallen man
The way He made was God's great plan
They put Him silent in the grave
Could the Word the lost ones save?
Yes, for from the grave He did rise
Beyond corruption to the skies
His words are heard, His truth remains
God's Son triumphant forevermore reigns

Tyrone Brown

Christ is Mine

His suffering was alone for sin
In anguish felt God's wrath within
The cross was God's salvation plan
His gift in love, to sinful man
Peace is mine because He gave
In grace His life, my soul to save
Personal trust is all that's required
Faith in Him, is what is desired
Christ is mine, with God's word as my trust
His security sure, but faith is a must
Lord Jesus Christ, He is precious to me
I look for the day when His face I will see

Tyrone Brown

His Promises

How through my life can I contend
With greatest strength, through to the end?
Finding hope in the truth of God's word
Walking with triumph, His ways we have learned
Taking our stand with our Saviour and friend
He's promised He's with us, through to the end
His power eternal never will fail
Through prayer, His strength I must of Him avail
Giving His promise His grace He will send
Pouring in blessing, through to the end
With assurance I sit, in His presence in peace
The answer to worry and my fears to release
His comfort is promised; broken hearts He will mend
He walks beside us, and will to the end

Tyrone Brown

In the Everlasting Arms

In the Everlasting Arms
With Christ in glory free from harm
Redeemed and perfect like his Lord
The song of glory to sing in accord
With wonder he looks on the Saviour's face
What joy it is to be in that place
No sickness or tears are cried in God's Heaven
Sin's curse is gone, he stands forgiven
Sorrow, knowing it's only a space
We soon shall all meet, saved by God's grace

Lyndon Brown

Israel

The eternal promise of God will stand
To give to Israel Canaan's land
With war and trouble this land is fraught
Rebellion and sin this suffering has brought
Written within God's prophetic scrolls
This gift will return to believing souls
This land which once saw miracles divine
Saw Jesus turn water to wine
Will one day see His feet descend
To destroy His enemies, and war will end
Israel will see their Messiah and King
Will bow in worship and His praises sing
They will look on the one with pierced hands and feet
His chosen people their God will meet
In blessing and joy they'll inherit the land
Their Messiah will rule with a righteous hand

Lyndon Brown

Israel

Promised Messiah, their God and King
This chosen people with Moses did sing
Pitching their tents in the wilderness
Calling on God in their times of distress
His love remained through famine and war
Providing them manna from Heaven's store
This people that journeyed saw God's mighty hand
Going to Canaan their divine promised land
Land of milk and honey that flowed
Land where the blessing of God was bestowed
Today this land with trouble is torn
The scriptures of this time did warn
It is the plan of God foretold
That Israel will their Messiah behold
This place of trouble, sorrow and pain
Will be the place where Christ will reign
The Messiah in power, will triumph in war
The ruler of Heaven their land will restore
Reigning with peace and perfect right
In the beauty of holiness and supreme delight

Tyrone Brown

Joy with Rejoicing

It is our theme with promised strength
With love that has no breadth or length
Unfailing joy; the greatest peace
Within our souls when strivings cease
Our Lord, His joy has filled our heart
Content in this, we'll never part
Praise with joy, our hearts should fill
Rejoicing is His mind and will
The greatest promise fulfilled in me
Joy with rejoicing through eternity

Tyrone Brown

Living Christ

I have in me the living Word
The power of my risen Lord
Present peace within my soul
Love and joy the Spirit's role
This life in Christ portrays God's grace
Portrays the love found in Christ's face
Producing fruit for Heaven's throne
The aspiration of His own
It is the hope of all who trust
His commendation is a must
To hear His words "Well done my son"
Eternal reward received from the one
Who is eternally, the Lord of all
The one before all people fall

Tyrone Brown

All Around

Looking up I'm given insight
Into Heaven's glory bright
Looking back I'm glad He came
God's Son chose to take my shame
Looking down I ever stumble
With great misery I grumble
Looking sideways my Lord beside me
Then I know His presence cheers me
Looking forward life's path God plans
The future is in better hands
The world around is His domain
The days we live are not in vain

Tyrone Brown

Mansions Prepared

You and I have mansions, not made with hands
The builder and maker is our Lord in that land
Eternal in the heavens, without sins curse to destroy
With thoughts of our presence He's preparing with joy
The home for His bride He has loved and redeemed
Prepared by the one who the Father esteemed
Worthy to sit on the throne there on high
His blood the token to cleanse and justify
His heavenly bride, His church, will bring home
We'll be there forever; no more shall we roam

Tyrone Brown

Prayer

I met my Lord in prayer today
He promised He will guide my way
The light He'll shine when paths seem dark
My course of life He's there to mark
He counts my hairs; He knows my thought
The blessings of life by Him are brought
In weakness I falter but He holds my hand
By His power divine, through storms I stand
Under His wing He'll protect me from harm
Guarding in love, with His outstretched arm
By His grace there is peace for my soul
Contentment is mine when He's in control
Directing my life is my Lord and friend
True and faithful, on Him I depend

Tyrone Brown

Mighty His Power

Mighty in His power to save
"Righteous One" His life He gave
Precious His blood, poured out for sin
The cleansing healing I needed within
Hope for eternity, with approval divine
His word has promised "They are mine"
I will never fall from His grasp
The Trinity has me in Their hands' clasp
There planted in my heart the seed
The Word of truth, with grace indeed
Power to save, the one who came down
My Saviour and Lord, with glory His crown

Tyrone Brown

The Babe Born to Save

Mild and meek, the babe born to save
Plan of our God, His eternal Son gave
"Light of the world" wrapped in swaddling bands
Yet incarnate God, with the world in His hands
The manger His bed, the stable His room
His triumph as deity, He rose from the tomb
Little child in form, His heart full of love
God's Spirit descended on Him as a dove
Hidden His power, this hope for mankind
The greatest gift given our soul can find

Tyrone Brown

Miracle of Grace

Hopeless, with no remedy or cure
The leper daily cried "Impure! Impure!"
His skin was spotted with disease and decay
Powerless to cleanse the uncleanness away
But the miracle came when Jesus he found
"Lord cleanse me!" he cried as he knelt on the ground
Love reached out His hand and touched this poor man
The God of Heaven had come with a plan
He spoke the word "Believe and be clean."
The leper was cleansed right there on the scene
Pure his body, but even greater his soul
Miracle of grace, his life was made whole

I was hopeless, with sin my disease
Choosing a path that myself I would please
Powerless to save myself from sin's chain
The life that was bound in fear and in pain
God's miracle came when Jesus I found
The chain was released when I knelt on the ground
The Saviour in love came to stretch out His hand
When He died for my sin, as His father had planned
The word He has spoken "Believe and be saved"
His way to the glory by His blood has been paved
My sins have been cleansed; the past is forgiven
Miracle of grace, eternal life God has given

Tyrone Brown

As Morning Dawns

Morning dawns with Heaven's light
The person of Christ shines in glory bright
Tears gone forever; the darkness is past
The joy in perfection experienced at last
The redeemed are singing with joy the great song
Worshipping their Saviour, to whom they belong
Washed and cleansed by the blood of the Lamb
As forgiven they fall before the great I Am
Hope of all who trust in God's word
As comfort to those who sorrow have learned

Tyrone Brown

My Hope

My hope isn't "maybe", uncertain or unsure
Its confident trust in Heaven that is sure
Precious blood is my certain passport to Heaven
The life of Christ, on the cross that was given
Powerless I stood outside of the door
My entrance barred, by my sin I deplore
But Christ in love, gave me hope in Him
Hope that's eternal, that never will dim
In time I stand, but my soul will live on
Thankful secure in the One who has gone
Into Heaven above, my home to prepare
Waiting with love for His bride to be there
This hope is mine, without worry or fear
This hope is found in my Saviour so dear

Tyrone Brown

Beloved Lord Jesus

My Lord is beloved; a master so kind
Provider of strength with His hand in mine
My path may seem hard but He leads the way
He has promised it leads to eternal day
Creator of all, but He's my best friend
Being my Saviour, on Him I depend
Morning Star, revealing His purpose
Greater light than the sun shining on us
He's coming triumphant, but first I will see
The one who loved me through eternity
The trumpet first sound will call me away
With my Heavenly redeemer forever to stay
Victor through suffering He is coming to reign
Then I will stand with His glorious train
This beloved Lord Jesus, changeless through time
Will continue forever in glory to shine

Tyrone Brown

No Condemnation

My need was met by God's own Son
In conquering death the victory was won
Condemned I stood before the law
Holiness demanded one without flaw
The condemnation - doomed to die
With nothing in me to justify
This hopeless state brought pain and fear
The binding chords grew year by year
Then through the darkness shone a light
Freedom found through Jesus' might
The man Christ Jesus stood in my place
The condemnation of sin did face
With righteousness He fulfilled the law
No sin in Him His Father saw
Triumphant in death His work was complete
Destroying the enemy with crushing defeat
His cleansing blood has brought me peace
His death the chords of sin released

Tyrone Brown

Priceless Blessing

Money cannot buy it, nor can a price be given
To the peace within my heart, from my Lord in Heaven
His boundless love has shed His light upon the path I tread
Light dispelling darkness, giving hope for life ahead
Though facing valleys deep with pain, or mountain tops of joy
The peace of God fills all my thoughts, and grace my heart enjoys
This life of peace and hope, has known forgiveness by God's grace
His blessings flow with righteousness; great hope I'll see His face

Tyrone Brown

Peace

The peace my soul is looking for
Oh can the Lord His peace restore?
The river ever flows in love
From His eternal throne above
Through sorrows, pain, and fears that storm
The character of strength will form
Patience through the seas of life
Peace He gives, though there is strife
The way can seem too hard to chart
But can He not His love impart?
In realms of spiritual thought His grace
Is given my fears to fight and to face
Ocean's waters are deep and dark
But His light the shore will mark
The Heavenly shore is where there's rest
Our haven in one who knows what's best
And so with hope in God's great love
I center my eyes on Heaven above
My lot in life may have its pains
But His strength always remains
There through the comfort of His word
The promise of His help is heard

Tyrone Brown

Perfect Peace

His peace is perfect, when I give Him control
Peace most present, when He dwells in my soul
The triumph is mine through faith in His Word
Personal power, through Christ, I have learned
Promises written, unlimited and free
Spoken by Christ, in love just for me
This hope delivers from the bondage of fear
Making Him wonderful, precious and dear
He smiles upon me through life's difficult ways
His presence within and His peace there it stays

Tyrone Brown

Place of Comfort

Place of comfort in God's care
The Lord alone, your burden will share
In love He comes, His child to bless
With hope and peace, in tenderness
He knows the sorrow in your heart
He knows the pain when loved ones part
But He gives hope, you'll meet again
Forever in Heaven, where there's no more pain
Depend on His word; the Lord will not fail
Through trial and suffering, His grace will prevail

Lyndon Brown

Peter

Until our Lord said "Follow me"
The fish he caught swam in the sea
Peter was called to fish for men
With passion and love as the Saviour had been
Only a fisherman, yet the power divine
He wrote a book revealing the sign
He'd been with Jesus, as a disciple and friend
The writing a miracle, as unlearned men
Were not equipped to read or write
Or walk on water in the night
Both were miracles only God can perform
The same as when He stilled the storm
Peter's faith failed in the test
But the Lord brought out his best
His life he laid down for his Lord
Power within from the Spirits sword
By the Word of God overcame the fear
Of weapons and men who would not hear
The gospel of Christ and the darkness of sin
How they needed salvation and cleansing within
Remember Peter, he was only a man
But when Christ he met a new life began

Lyndon Brown

Plans of Our God

Plans of our God in times past must be seen
The fulfillment of prophesies that spoken had been
The Saviour in human form must be found
A perfect man, where sin's darkness abounds
Bethlehem chosen as place for His birth
The manger His bed, as He lay on this earth
He never had a kingly crown
Though wisemen worshipped and gifts they lay down
As He sat with intelligent men
The child with wisdom answered yet again
My Father has work He wants me to do
I must to His word and commandment be true
He had compassion as He looked on their tears
He calmed the sea and quelled their fears
This life which was holy, to Calvary went
To pay for our ransom; for sin it was spent
He triumphed with truth, as He rose from the grave
He was God's Son, who had come to save
To Heaven ascended, seated now on the throne
Power, glory and honour He receives from his own

Lyndon Brown

Real Peace

I wandered through the forest pines
Away from the town's social confines
The hush of nature's peace and calm
Reminded me of David's Psalm
In quietness, I know God's there
His promise is "I'll always care"
The presence of my Lord I feel
His peace within I know is real.

Lyndon Brown

Refiners Fire

Life of gold refined and pure
The value eternal; in Christ it's secure
There must be fire to bring out the best
The Christian must pass through the heat of the test
Fiery trials that seem too hard to bear
But our Lord knows our path and watches with care
With love, He allows the hurt and the pain
The suffering felt again and again
His heart knows the feelings as one who's been there
Through His path on this earth He is fully aware
Touched by our feelings, His love reaches down
To comfort and whisper "In Heaven's your crown"
Purified with value more precious than gold
His purpose in Glory will forever unfold

Tyrone Brown

Rejoice Evermore

With each passing moment we are told to rejoice
Reason to sing and lift up our voice
We are redeemed, and a child of the King
Precious our Saviour and His great offering
Praying continually, we're in His presence divine
With His promise of hearing, since He said "You are mine"
We feel His peace, and in this we can rest
Knowing He'll answer and by Him be blessed
Giving of thanks is the greatest use of our mind
It overcomes thoughts of the negative kind
Positive source, it always brings joy
With knowing the Lord has given us all we enjoy
These are the ways to give glory and praise
Doing God's will and filling our days
Rejoicing and praying, with thanksgiving in our heart
The appreciation we feel will set us apart

Lyndon Brown

Remembering Jesus

Remembering Jesus; a pilgrim to earth
Almighty God in humble birth
Lord of lords, yet in a manger He lay
Shepherds worshipped this one in the hay
Wisemen brought gifts, coming from far
Announcing His coming – in the heavens a star

As a child He sat with those of the law
Throughout His life, He was without flaw
This one stilled storms, gave blind their sight
Raised the dead by God's own might
But preaching truth soon had Him bound
Truth that men's hearts in sin were found

With nails they pierced God's only son
Even though only great kindness He'd done
But it was the fulfilment of God's plan to save
Showing His love, His wondrous son gave
This same Jesus rose with power divine
With glory and majesty in Heaven He shines

Lyndon Brown

The Author of Salvation

Wearing the title "Finisher," His work is complete
The triumph, the Victor will never repeat
This salvation eternal will forever abide
Unfailing security when "Finished" He cried
The life He has given now frees us to live
Patience with power His Spirit will give
The Author has written the title in love
His authority confirmed by the Father above
In faith we look to Jesus the "Word"
The eternal message through Him we have learned

Tyrone Brown

The Carpenter's Hands

Only was an instrument pounding nails into wood
Pounded by the carpenter who formed the trees that stood
Outside the city on the hill, where forests shade the sun
The founder of the universe, the one who was God's Son
Through hammering and forming wood, made simple wooden things
Yet these hands had formed the world and universe that sings
The pounding of each nail gave thoughts, of His suffering
The nails that would pierce His hands, and mans rejection bring
The hands of a carpenter were the hands that gave sight
Resurrected the dead and brought us God's light
The hands that once were, outstretched in love
Present pierced hands, to God the Father above

Tyrone Brown

God of Truth

The God of truth we want to know
His Son, the Christ, His life did show
Eternal the Word, eternal the Son
Infinite love in the work that was done
Though He died in our stead, sins curse He bore
The power of death unlocked evermore
Through Jesus my Saviour not only I live
But His peace and joy He's promised to give
Daily I learn God's life, joy and peace
Life that has given sin's captive release
Eternal life, in knowing His grace
Forever I'll worship when I look on His face

Tyrone Brown

The Man Christ Jesus

Protector in storms of life that assail
Divine in His power; He will always prevail
Our security proven through His power over wind
Rebuking the storm; His might did transcend
With complete control He preserves us from harm
With His competent help there's no need for alarm
Having spoken the world into orbit through Word
He created the universe when His voice was heard
Eternal in power but became finite man
The Man Christ Jesus; God's Son "the Lamb"

Tyrone Brown

The Race

Not what is past but what is ahead
Life is not stagnant but a challenge instead
The race is not run by the one without heart
It only is won, seeing the goal from the start
Not the prize of worldly gain
Not success of wealth and fame
The goal is the One who has run on before
He secured the prize when my sins He bore
The high calling of God is the goal of the race
The prize to win, to look on Christ's face

Tyrone Brown

The Eternal Word

There is infinite power in Heaven's great Light
Creator, designer, with transcending might
The foundations of all He laid with a plan
Before He breathed life into the very first man

Angels, His ministers, give anthems of praise
To the Lord of all; the Ancient of Days
Voice of the universe thundered command
He spoke the word and chaos became land

His power so awesome, but love greater still
As the infinite one came, the law to fulfill
The revealer of eternity and Heaven's high throne
Came through manifold wisdom to redeem His own

Though men bound Him in chords and led Him away
His purpose was manifest; they must have their way
The cross, though a curse, was God's holy demand
Sin's curse brought judgement and death His command

Being our substitute He paid the great price
His death all sufficient; the supreme sacrifice
With victorious power He conquered the grave
This wondrous deliverer lost souls came to save

As conqueror, to Heaven's grand throne He ascended
Fulfilling all righteousness and the truth He defended
Glory, honour and power throughout Heaven is heard
Worshipping the one who eternally is the Word

Tyrone Brown

The Greatest Gift

This gift from Heaven, in Mary's arms lay
The Son of God chose a manger of hay
Born in a stable but Creator of all
Heavenly one, but answered God's call
"Who will go for sinners lost?
Who will pay the awful cost?"
"Here am I send me" He said
"I will go die in their stead"
So He came as perfect man
Humble servant, in God's plan
His mother watched His hands of grace
Saw blind eyes see His lovely face
She inwardly knew the man was divine
He had power to turn water to wine
The sea, though tossed, calmed by His word
His voice in power His disciples heard
But for our sin, was why He came
To take the curse and death of shame
Mary saw Him lifted up
Watched Him drink that bitter cup
Full of sorrow, she walked away
But found He'd risen on the third day
His ascension she watched as to Heaven He went
To be the Savior of the world was why He was sent

Tyrone Brown

He Cares

Troubles come but Someone cares
A Friend who all our burdens shares
He promises He's always there
Completely on Him you can rest your care
Great God He is, and Father too
He'll strengthen, heal and uplift you

Tyrone Brown

We Beheld His Glory

Truth revealed in one perfect man
Hidden in him, God's eternal plan
Presenting the God who cannot lie
Fulfilling God's promises He came to die
In Christ the Word, the Father was seen
Very essence of God; the one who's supreme
Born sinless, the Creator, Gods glory displayed
Mind of the Godhead, incarnate was made
Unmerited favour His thoughts were in grace
Redeeming poor sinners by taking their place
His life shone His glory, in power and might
His father declared "in Him is all my delight"

Tyrone Brown

His Care

Under His eye we are watched from above
He guides us each step, with a father's love
Pointing us in the way we should take
Cheering our soul when our heart seems to break
Reaching His hand to lift us up
Giving living water to fill our cup
As infinite showers of blessings He pours
There speaks peace and assurance from His abundant stores
The harbour of safety when troubles come
Always beside us as our race is run
We are never alone as we have His word
Safe in His care is what we have learned

Lyndon Brown

For unto us a child is born, unto us a son is given: and the government shall be upon his shoulder and his name shall be called Wonderful, Counselor, The mighty God, the everlasting Father and the Prince of Peace.

Isaiah 9:6

Unto Us a Child is Born

The Son of God was always there
Was found a child; our sins would bare
Upon His shoulder the government would be
Ruling through time in sovereignty
With God's unswerving purpose He came
Divine in person, deserving His name
Heaven's answer to this sin cursed earth
The Wonderful one of unspeakable worth
The Counselor, so wise and true
Apparent to all, as a child He grew
Almighty God, powerful with might
Resurrection from death His God given right
Father of Eternity, through endless ages will reign
Redeeming His own through suffering and pain
Delivering our souls from bondage and grief
The Prince of Peace, gives poor sinners relief

Lyndon Brown

Hope Holds the Key

Unfailing is our Lord's design
Though fear and doubt may fill my mind
With promise for my good He moves
Throughout my life as He must choose
The plan, both soul and body takes
Directs my path with no mistakes
Loving care His power displays
As He guides through difficult ways
His promise is sure it will not fail
Hope holds the key as the plan He'll unveil

Tyrone Brown

Victory

Great is our Captain, triumphant in war
He won the battle when our sins He bore
With triumph He rose, with God's power over death
Witness to the claim He gave man the first breath
This leader in spiritual warfare ascended on high
With His conquest completed, we never will die
As our defender He gives power to fight
The powers of darkness which hinder the light
Giving deliverance, the victory is ours
His promise which keeps us through trials dark hours
The battle is over, for the faith we contend
The crown of righteousness for His glory, our end

Tyrone Brown

Waters of Time

Under the waters of time, God carves our purpose in life
We know the river winds through valleys of trouble and strife
There rain and storm overflow its banks, with floods intended to prove
The Spirit of God is guiding and teaching us the way that we should move
The winds dry, with unstoppable force, the affliction of the hurting soul
Through the warmth of sunlight from Heaven, the love of God consoles
He knows what is needed to widen our banks, to spread the gospel story
His purpose in carving our life's river is to bring Him honour and glory

Lyndon Brown

The Babe in the Hay

What do you think of the babe in the hay?
The beacon of hope in the manger did lay
Is He only respected as one
That Mary called her sweet little son?
This baby, shepherds did come to behold
The king of the Jews, wisemen were told
Have you thought of the reason He came?
The meaning of "Jesus", His God given name?
This man who preached was the Heavenly Word
The man who all the multitudes heard
Have you cared that for sinners He came?
That today He is calling your name?
"Come unto me" He gives rest to the soul
Beyond all thought, while ages shall roll
Did He go to the cross for you?
Completing salvation; there is nothing to do
Has He risen and eternally lives?
That hope and peace to believers he gives
This babe in the manger we remember just now
The Heavenly child; to Him every knee will bow
His salvation He gives as a free gift to all
Will you trust in Him now and answer His call?

Tyrone Brown

Who is this Jesus?

Who is this Jesus in the manger bed
Who is this one to whom wisemen were led
Who is this baby who gave angels a song
Who is this one to whom praise belongs
Who is the one shepherds bowed before
Who is this one Mary and Joseph adore
Who is this Jesus who was given this name
Who is this one "God's son" can claim

This one in the manger is Creator of all
This one every person before Him will fall
This one is God's only well beloved son
This one has finished the work He begun
This one is the Light and is the Way
This one only, sin's debt could pay
This is the Saviour, who came from above
This one, "incarnate God", is love

Lyndon Brown

The Christmas Story

Who was this Jesus - center of history's dates?
What gave Him this place the world celebrates?
The Bible contains His most wonderful story
Now let us portray it and give Him the glory

In Heaven, with His Father on high
By His word with power, He spread the sky
Creating all, He chose a plan
A plan before the world began
He spoke the word and it was done
This one was God's eternal Son
Adam He made; He wanted a friend
But sin in the garden brought this to an end
This caused Him pain, the curse it brought
Death – this formed His very thought
I must become a perfect man
I must fulfill my eternal plan

Nothing deterred His heart to fulfill
The promises He made, through the prophets quill
He would be born, the prophet wrote
This verse from Isaiah we often quote

"For unto us a child is born, unto us a son is given and the government
shall be upon his shoulder; and his name shall be called Wonderful,
Counsellor, the Mighty God, the Everlasting Father, the Prince of Peace."
Isaiah 9:6

Mary was chosen to be the one
To deliver God's beloved Son
Zachariah was told in the temple one day
His son would be born to prepare the way
For this child from Heaven to bring life and light
To give men in darkness their spiritual sight

"The people that walked in darkness have seen a great
light. They that dwell in the land of the shadow of
death, upon them hath the light shined. Isaiah 9:2"

Mary betrothed to Joseph so kind
God spoke to him of Heaven's mind
Joseph was told His name would be
"Jesus " the Saviour, to set us free
With Bethlehem chosen, David's city the place
They came through the night to find no space
The inns were all full, with no room for the pair
The stable with animals, their stalls they would share
The baby was born, as animals watched on
This Creator of all, human form had donned

Reason to sing, the angels heralded His birth
They sang in chorus "Peace on earth"
With the song of His glory the heavens rang out
Shepherds heard it with wonder; there is no doubt
They feared the sight of the Heavenly host
Then heard the news and left their post
They found the babe in a manger of hay
Bowing down before Him, their worship to pay
Wrapped in His bands of earths cotton cloth
Without fancy ribbons and frilly froth
In humble place God's Son was found
Lowly manger His cradle; our thoughts it astounds
How can we measure the stoop that brought Light
Into this world, found in sin's darkest night?

Then in proclamation of the King of all kings
Had been born in Bethlehem and salvation He brings
Wisemen saw a special star
They came to see Him from afar
The star shone above Jesus house in the night
When they came they said "We have seen a great light"
To worship they came, bringing gifts to the King
Gold, frankincense and myrrh is what they did bring
God incarnate, had come to save
To conquer sin, death and the grave

Jesus grew with wisdom through time
Holy – faultless – righteous - sublime
He healed the sick in critical health
He lived in poverty; He had no wealth
His mother knew His divine power
God's son who created the beautiful flower
His miracles proved His deity
His life was lived in purity
Then to the cross He went in shame
They rejected the one whose very name
Told of salvation, and God's great plan
His souls desire to save fallen man
Triumphant over death and the grave
He rose in victory, our souls to save

Who is this Jesus, Christmas is all about?
The Son of God - there is no doubt

Tyrone Brown

Founded in Christ

With fountains of blessings the Lord has bestowed
Riches and wealth more precious than gold
A family proud of your care and devotion
Your love as a lighthouse beaming out on the ocean
The waves of time have pounded the rocks
But your faith has stood firm, as with God you talk
Powerful in force the water is moving
Your prayers have been answered as the Lord you've been proving
As diamonds sparkle across the sunlit sea
Your blessing to your family shines endlessly
Though winds may blow and life's storms may roar
Above it all, together you soar
We paint a picture we love to view
A picture of love that stands strong and true

Lyndon Brown

Word of Life

Word of Life within my heart lives
So abundant the joy and peace that He gives
As sun to the flowers, growing in spring
His light spreads His love abroad, so I sing
The wonder that Christ was willing to die
Was alone in the darkness to ask "Why, oh why?"
What grace and mercy redeeming the lost
What salvation He gives at such a great cost
With righteous forgiveness, I sing out His praise
As flowers in the garden their fragrant scent raise
Worship ascends from my heart to His name
To the Word of Life, who from Heaven came

Lyndon Brown

Past, Present and Future

Yesterday prayed for God's peace in my soul
Feeling the tempest and out of control
Present within, the Spirit whispers His peace
Giving me comfort with such boundless release
When I am anxious, the Word of God is my calm
Preserving my mind as I read in the Psalms
Like rivers refreshing, God's promises renew
My faith and my hope, as the fresh morning dew
Prayer provides the strength, to overcome each day
The power for my weakness, and Jesus Christ display

Tyrone Brown

Just a Sinner Saved by Grace

Just a sinner saved by grace
One day soon I'll see Christ's face
Found in His unsullied light
His perfection my delight

One with him our song we raise
Worthy to receive our praise
Trophies of his grace and love
Glory to our Lord above

Without sin redeemed and pure
My salvation is secure
Not my works of kindness done
But the work of God's dear Son

Lyndon Brown

Wonder of Wonders

Mighty God came to bring peace to the earth
Hope of the ages, incarnate in birth
With angels proclaiming the glorious news
The Redeemer had come, the way God did choose
More than a baby in a manger of hay
Deity swaddled, there in humility lay
Pleasing the Father the eternal Word came
Born in a stable, with "Jesus" His name
The Saviour of all; His purpose was clear
His name declared the work He had here
Prince of Peace; the Creator of all
Yet His cradle was the animal's stall
Wonder of wonders the Saviour came
The Son of God, who is ever the same

Tyrone Brown

Faith is a Must

More help to trust my Lord in Heaven
His hope and grace to me be given
I falter and stumble, weak in my walk
Prayer is my strength when with him I talk
Spirit my comfort, within is his grace
To be my guide as difficulties I face
In life the path may not be straight
Perhaps there seems bars lock the gate
But miracles are His; He always performs
He comes to my aid as I pass through life's storms
His strength is mine when on him I trust
Having more faith in him is a must

Tyrone Brown

The Great Commission

More voices to go into the world to preach
So many are lost, with a soul to reach
Hope is our message, with mercy and grace
Hope found alone in Christ's loving face
Telling the gospel with sincerity and love
Doing the work of our Father above
We are responsible to spread the good news
To go to the field that our Lord would choose
The God who has saved us will give us His strength
His power that has no breadth and no length
His promise to bless will never be broken
Believe there is power in every word spoken
Blessing His word, there'll be fruit to be seen
Salvation of souls where the gospel has been
Commissioned to go with the truth so divine
Going into the darkness to let our light shine
Glorifying our Saviour, our praise to His name
His gospel resounding, it's eternally the same

Tyrone Brown

Joseph

God planned his life before his birth
His parents pride and present worth
A special coat of colours sewn
His brothers wished it was their own
Their jealous poison destroyed their hearts
They sold their brother for silver parts
His poor soul cried as freedom gone
They bound his hands "Oh this is wrong"
In Egypt found the servant be
To Potiphar obediently
Gods hand in all his actions moved
Though troubles often trying proved
He made the most of prison though
He couldn't prove the lie was so
Fortune was God had him there
The butler and the baker pair
With dreams they needed both to know
God gave interpretation so
The butler could to pharaoh give
The name of Joseph for to live
The dreams of pharaoh then he saw
As God told him true given law
To take the grain and corn in store
The famine meant they would implore
The king to feed the starving land
He needed Joseph to give a hand
Now on the throne beside the king
The people did their money bring
Hoping to have their children fed
His brothers came to Egypt for bread
Then bowing down God's dream fulfilled
Their sacks by Joseph then were filled
But in that sack his cup he put

The brothers made to take a look
The cup was there inside the sack
Reason given for them to come back
His brother Benjamin he must see
Their only enemy now was he
Their father pleaded for his son
No good they might have ever done
Instead of right they knew to do
They made up stories that were not true
Giving consent the brothers took
More money and gifts that made them look
Poor Israelites without bread, not spies
This they knew he thought were lies
Binding the goods they made their way
Back to Joseph to give their pay
Their brother Simeon now was free
The banquet laid so plentifully
Now Joseph sent all others out
Giving his name, he left no doubt
With his brothers he reasoned why
Gods plan for them that they not die
The hope renewed of father's sight
He sent for him with great delight
Hearing his son was living free
Jacob cried so happily
The years had passed with sorrow true
The reunion now he must pursue
How none would know the joy he felt
When before his son he knelt
Now Joseph knew God's plan complete
Giving instruction for bones to meet
The land that God had promised to
The chosen people of Israel true

Tyrone Brown

His Flock He Leads (tune: Oh Danny Boy)

With ways of grace He leads his flock to waters still
With patient love He watches over them
His sheep He feeds as with His Word He them will fill
Their hearts with God's great wisdom, truth and love
Unlimited the fountain flows from Christ above
With all His wondrous peace poured over them
Eternally, salvation will preserve His own
The Shepherd Great to pastures green will lead His flock

Lyndon Brown

Esteeming the reproach of Christ greater riches than the treasures in Egypt...

Hebrews 11:26

Heaven's Riches

Gain the riches of this earth
With knowledge of its present worth
But can those riches dare compare
With Heaven's glories that are there
In radiant beauty our mansion's prepared
With all in perfection and nothing repaired
Salvation though is greater treasure
Eternal life with Christ can we measure?
The wealth of God's tremendous love
In sending His Son down from above
No, the things of life will perish
But the gifts eternal forever we'll cherish

Tyrone Brown

He Holds the Key

The door is locked; who holds the key?
Entry is barred; how can I be free?
Hope beckons me on though the way seems blocked
The one who saved me will see it unlocked
Strength is small, the body weak
The road ahead can seem so bleak
But God is great and his power divine
His strength he promises will be mine
He opened the door it cannot be closed
Regardless of what many others supposed
The challenge, my focus as onward I go
The one who holds the key, I know
Yes the door is now open I have freedom to run
The race before me until it is won

Tyrone Brown

His Strength

It isn't alone I have strength to live free
To overcome worry and anxiety in me
There is strength in the one who knows my heart
Living within, His power He imparts
Though I stumble, and might lose control
The Spirit of God whispers peace to my soul
As fear and doubt take me down in despair
The promise of God says "I will always be there"
Regardless the circumstance I must trust without doubt
The way to find peace, moving negative thoughts out
It is with prayer, power over worry is found
Casting cares on my Lord the joy will abound

Tyrone Brown

Hope of Glory

Prepared in Heaven our eternal home
Present with Christ no more to roam
Forever living; no separation there
Tears are dried in a morning so fair
The night is passed; darkness dispelled
The glory removes the sadness that dwelled
Within our hearts, that trials brought
The curse of death and sin we fought
In the presence of the one who is Love
The hope of glory, in Heaven above

Tyrone Brown

Peace In the Storm

Peace in seas with waves of care
The peace which comes alone from prayer
Waters pound the shores of life
Harsh winds blow with trials and strife
But my Lord speaks through the storm
"My peace I give; you see my form
I stand upon the raging seas
From me the fierce storm calms and flees
This peace I leave to give you calm
I hold you fast within my palm"
I have His word "Be not afraid"
I have my care before Him laid
My troubled heart has found through trust
Real peace in Christ, but faith's a must

Tyrone Brown

Clothed in Righteousness

Righteousness clothes me since I have believed
Christ now indwells me since Him I've received
Wonder eternal, I'll be in the presence of God
Loved and forgiven since Christ bore the rod
Powerless I was, to cleanse all my sin
The cleansing I've found since He washed me within
Made pure through the blood of His cross
Divine deliverance since He suffered such loss
Prepared, a mansion in Heaven for me
Promise of Christ since my soul He set free
My shield and defence with His Word as my sword
Hope and salvation since trusting in Jesus my Lord

Tyrone Brown

Power Through Christ

Patiently enduring the conflicts of life
As pressures rise and the disturbing strife
Of disbelief and personal pain
The constant fight is not in vain
Inner peace has had its way
Though troubles come from day to day
This battleground of life's silent voice
The disability without a choice
This place of discord but also calm
Is found in God's eternal palm
Power to overcome the thought
Of fear and worry weakness brought
Alone is in Christ's strength poured in
With his promise with him I'll win

Lyndon Brown

On the Way to Emmaus

Morning came with sadness wrought
Their Lord was dead, or so they thought
Israel's redeemer, they had been sure
Three days passed; they felt insecure
But as they made their way and walked
His presence came and with them talked
Expounding to them God's salvation plan
His foundation was to become a man
The Hope of Heaven; the only Way
Power and love He did display
God's Son had come to die for sin
His life was given, their souls to win
With eyes in sadness and unbelief
They couldn't see because of grief
They invited Him in to stay awhile
He had walked with them the extra mile
Then as He prayed, Christ was revealed
His wounds of Calvary could not be concealed
They sat in awe of their Lord they had seen
Helpless to understand how blind they had been
His presence lifted concern, without trust
With His hands still wounded, their faith was a must
As the two on the way to Emmaus had found
The Lord with His word, His plan did expound
We have to walk with our Lord to know
His plans for us and the way to go
His presence is with us; He never forsakes
Even though sadly, we make many mistakes
Going through life He walks along side
When we invite Him in, He'll with us abide

Tyrone Brown

Peter

Until our Lord said "Follow me"
The fish he caught swam in the sea
Peter was called to fish for men
With passion and love as the Saviour had been
Only a fisherman, yet the power divine
He wrote a book revealing the sign
He'd been with Jesus, as a disciple and friend
The writing a miracle, as unlearned men
Were not equipped to read or write
Or walk on water in the night
Both were miracles only God can perform
The same as when He stilled the storm
Peter's faith failed in the test
But the Lord brought out his best
His life he laid down for his Lord
Power within from the Spirits sword
By the Word of God overcame the fear
Of weapons and men who would not hear
The gospel of Christ and the darkness of sin
How they needed salvation and cleansing within
Remember Peter, he was only a man
But when Christ he met a new life began

Lyndon Brown

The Pearl of Great Price

So precious to God, this pearl of great worth
He paid the price when Christ came to this earth
The value He placed on sinners like me
Cost Christ the suffering of Calvary's tree
So great the price He gave His all
Almighty God found in a manger stall
Why such value in my sinful soul?
Why would He pay such an awful toll?
The love He had, found Him paying the cost
Of the judgement of sin; condemned to be lost
Wonder of wonders God paid for the pearl
The value to Him through eternity will unfurl

Lyndon Brown

Forever My Friend

Yesterday, today and forever, my Friend He'll always be
He'll never leave me comfortless or turn His back on me
My friend is God, so He can never change
My life and my pathway, He will ever arrange
His presence my comfort, and peace to my soul
When my thoughts rage, He is there to console
Yesterday, before there was light
He was with me with strength, to win my fight
Today He is with me, with assurance and calm
He has said in His Word, I am held in His palm
He has promised to keep me, every day to the end
He's my Saviour and Lord, on whom I depend
He's closer than a brother, staying right at my side
Unchanging is His character; forever with me He'll abide

Tyrone Brown

The Saviour

In God's eternal plan, His birth
With love He came for us on earth
Became a man so He could be
The Saviour, so we can be free
God's son, yet human form He took
Contained within His holy book
Very God, in a manger of hay
There in a stable in humility lay
Promise of hope and salvation for all
Jesus, the name his parents would call
The Saviour He was, and forever will be
Cradled by Mary - divine Deity

Tyrone Brown

The Lord of Glory

Son of man, yet Son of God
He came in poverty, as his feet this earth trod
With wisdom eternal he knew God's plan
He veiled his glory to become a man
Very God incarnate, with power and might
Worship and glory his God given right
For sinners he came, in love and in grace
Showing compassion, as his steps we retrace
To Calvary's cross he went for our sin
Suffering anguish, from God's wrath within
Eternally God, his triumph was sure
The price was paid; salvation secure
His ascension in glory to Heaven's grand throne
Worship and praise he receives from his own
Crowned with glory, we all shall sing
Honour and majesty to Christ our king

Lyndon Brown

The Journey of Life

Life is a journey, everyone knows
Travel prepared, with guidance as we go
Through mountain passes and valley lows
The Word of God shields us from our foes
Prayer will keep us on the course
The Spirit of God, His strength our source
With Christ the Way our path is clear
He walks beside us, a friend so dear
The journey is planned with blessings in store
Trust in our Lord, who lives evermore

Tyrone Brown

Victory In Christ

Power comes through Christ alone
To fight the foe to which I'm prone
The foe of unbelief and fear
Its voice that whispers in my ear
"Nothing can be done through you
You're weak, and powerless, and hopeless too"
But words of strength then come to mind
Words of hope, the positive kind
"I will pour my strength within
To conquer weakness, fear and sin"
My war is conquered with prayer and belief
Victory in Christ, with peace and relief

Tyrone Brown

The Eternal Plan

See our flowers; spring is here
Wandering under our tree, a deer
Awesome beauty, God's creative hand
Causes wonder, how this earth He planned
But greater still His eternal plan
With love to save poor ruined man
He sacrificed His perfect Son
To give us joy; our strength and sun
Wonder of wonders, the God of all grace
Comfort and peace reveals in Christ's face

Lyndon Brown

Peace in Times of Troubled Seas

Peace in times of troubled seas
The Christian finds upon his knees
Though winds of trials blow a gale
Through strength in prayer, he will prevail
With storm clouds hiding the rays of light
In Christ His Lord his hope is bright
Waves of doubt may toss the ship
But faith remains; he keeps his grip
God's answer comes and calms the seas
The power to trust, found on his knees

Lyndon Brown

A Praying Mother

A mother praying with her heart, in love
With faith, to God her Father who sits in Heaven above
Her prayer is mindful of her children's cares
God alone the burden fully shares
The pain she sees her children going through
Their worries, hurt, their trials and insecurity too
Pouring out their needs, to one who's always there
With full assurance in faith, this one will always care
Her children are held up, before the Throne of Grace
Their struggles that they fight, and worry that they face
The love of a mother who believes God will hear
This one is called "blessed", by her children she holds dear

Tyrone Brown

Peace in Prayer

In peace of mind will hope be found
The happiness that the negative drowned
In thoughts of sadness and "woe is me"
The flood of doubt grows continuously
Waves of fear and pain assail
But God's strength can still prevail
Without faith the Spirit grieves
But prayer is trust and my heart believes
Divine protection since in me He lives
The promise to help surely He gives
But I must let Him control
My mind which seems without console
His peace can calm my troubled thought
When my despair to Him is brought

Tyrone Brown

The Victor

His visage marred; God's Son the one
Not His wrong, that this was done
Pain beyond our human thought
His dreadful form with anguish wrought
Unrecognized, the Nazarene
The friend of sinners He had been
God's Son was found in judgement hall
Though found in Him no fault at all
Pouring wrath out on His soul
The cry was heard without console
"Why have you forsaken me?"
The Word made sin for you and me
The wicked were there, when He died on the tree
They did not believe that Christ He could be
Our penalty paid; His death was complete
Never again will God's Son this repeat
The rich man laid Him in his tomb which was new
There had been no violence in Him they knew
With bruise, my sin by God was laid
The debt of sin was fully paid
With triumph He rose; with victory crowned
God's Son in Heaven now is found
The spoils of battle He is going to share
With His redeemed; those whose sins He did bare

Tyrone Brown

Thoughts from the Heart

Lives More than can be Understood

The blinds are closed. No one is home.
Who makes a peep? That gives the clue.
What lives inside that empty house?
That seems so abandoned and alone?
Behind those covered window shades
Lives more than can be understood.

The covered awning shades the porch
With accents of colour the flowers close in
The path to the door is hardly worn
Who visits a house where no one is home?
Behind the door can be so lonely
When lives more than can be understood.

With paint that is faded with passing of time
The building still stands; the foundation is firm.
Gutters don't leak when storms pour down rain
Heat of the sun warms the house within
Life on the inside has shut out the storms
Inside lives more than can be understood.

There lives behind that covered house
Beneath the weathered roof, still good
What others think, an empty shell
Aging with time but still growing strong
The one who's still silent, wishing each day
The house to be opened; to be understood.

Tyrone Brown

Lyndon Brown – age 3

Wounded Bird

Wounded bird, without power to fly
Wishing that one day he'd reach the sky
Taken by most as unable to rise
His intelligence and thoughts they seemed to despise
Weak and helpless he sat on the side
Hoping his dreams would not be denied
They wouldn't take time to give him a chance
Though when he wrote his eyes would dance
The pain in silence so hard to bear
His hurt inside he could not share
Poor wounded bird, but the story's not done
Strength within grew with the warmth of the sun
The Creator and Lord had plans for this one
Untying the wraps, which disbelief spun
Through patience and trust, acceptance and care
Gentleness began healing the hurt and despair
Hope was now bright as upward he gazed
Receiving honours through writing – the bird was amazed
With wings now healed the bird can now fly
Taking flight to reach his dreams in the sky
He may have been wounded, but freedom has come
Purpose in living and truth has won

Lyndon Brown

Tyrone Brown – age 9

The Silent Voice

Only could call by his crying and noise
He could not even play with the other boys
The hearing that he had no thought
Constantly frustration brought
He had no way to put them right
Until age eight when he could write
He typed his thoughts with someone's aid
Then found that teachers thought he played
They did not believe the work his own
His intelligence was overthrown
Having only pain he fought
With fear and anxiety his mind was fraught
But as he prayed his Lord could give
The strength for him to hope and live
These negative things that put him down
With power his positive thoughts did drown
Showing trust through their belief
Through high school years he found relief
These educators let him learn
His grades they knew he worked to earn
Though others would not hear his cries
He through this poem to them replies
The label you give has potential to harm
It is more than a name that gives cause for alarm
It defines a child for the person he is
But sadly may not be who he really is

Tyrone Brown

The Seed

The seed was planted in the garden of time
Planted as a child being read nursery rhymes
There it lay buried, covered and still
No gardener coming to hoe and to till
Dormant and silent the seed in the ground
Yet there was life waiting just to be found
Gathering weeds kept growing on top
Wasting good land that should have been crop
Then one day the plough removed all the weeds
Giving hope to the silent, buried, young seed
The gardener began watering the ground where it lay
The earth was warmed with the sun's bright ray
Out of the earth the silent seed grew
As a beautiful flower with all that it knew
It blossomed with flowers others never had seen
The plant growing strong that dormant had been
The gard'ner had taught so much to this flower
It bloomed with life and belief gave it power

Lyndon Brown

A Mother's Love

With mother's love she rocks her small baby
Pacifying him with care and devotion
With mother's love she walks with her child
Protecting this one as her most valued possession
With mother's love she teaches her boy
Preparing him for the road ahead
With mother's love she guides her son
Preserving him from the pitfalls of life
With mother's love she watches this man
Providing him with encouraging words
With mothers love she cherishes this gift
Praying the Lord will bless him with peace

Tyrone Brown

Friends

Friends know your feelings and are always there
To help when you need them and show that they care
They take time to talk, and listen as you speak
Talking of your challenges which leave you feeling weak
They are strength when you're stumbling, and wrestling with fear
Their presence will lift you and their smile will cheer
Depend on their guidance when uncertain of your course
They'll always encourage but their ideas never force
Respect and openness will characterize who they are
They will always be with you, even from far
Friends have your back and never turn away
They will ever be caring and are trusted to stay

Lyndon Brown

A Smile

It's only a smile but universal its power
Understood without words, like a red rose flower
Something so small reaches right to the heart
As sadness melts and sorrows depart
Though words aren't spoken so much is said
Acceptance and friendship as the smile is read
Written in language we all can share
There is no sign with which to compare
With the silence of a smile we all can speak
Whether great or small; whether strong or weak

Lyndon Brown

Apple Tree

She stands alone in many yards
Her blossoms are as a picture card
With beautiful flowers adorned in spring
As a bride covered with white veiling
Her perfume with a soft sweet smell
Wafts over the garden weaving a spell
The fruit she bears she asks you pick
Apples abound among leaves so thick
Then autumn as a cloud descends
Upon her boughs as summer ends
She sheds her leaves among the grass
She will now wait for winter to pass
Snow will cover her as she sleeps
Then in the spring small buds will peep

Lyndon Brown

Autumn

Peaceful scenes in golden hue
The grass is wet with heavy dew
The mist lies over the valley floor
The corn fields cut; put up in store
In place of flowers pumpkins rest
Among the trees are empty nests
Autumn closes summer's blind
Yet summer's mem'ries are left behind
In colour the Artist creation portrays
God's painted his world in so many ways

Lyndon Brown

Blossom I Love

The pretty flower wears the season's best style
Her colours are beautiful with the radiant smile
The fragrance of sweetness fills the air that I breathe
The perfume of love around me she weaves
Her foliage shelters my head from the sun
Spreading her leaves out as arms, for her son
Under the earth her roots go down deep
These preserve strength and her spirit they keep
With this strength, she's devoted and sure
Her children are blessed with a love that is pure
In the garden of life this beautiful flower
Grows in my heart as a bright yellow sunflower

Lyndon Brown

Canada

A place that we can call our home
A country where the wildlife roam
Crossing a continent from shore to shore
This land past voyagers came to explore
Its landscape with beauty captures our heart
Perpetually changing as the seasons depart
The prairies stretch in golden hue
As fields of wheat lie where prairie grass grew
The rolling hills overlooked by high mountains
Are watered by rivers from the snow melting fountains
In majestic beauty the great fir trees stand
While the ocean pounds the Pacific sand
Sounding its power the Atlantic roars
Shaping the land on our Maritime shores
Planting their roots the maple trees grow
Gorgeous in colour their leaves seem to glow
The lakes in abundance are shimmering jewels
While up in the north snow always rules
This land that is ours we must always cherish
Protecting its beauty, never letting it perish

Lyndon Brown

Free to Fly

Free beyond the hurt with fear
To fly with cloudless skies above
No frustration binding thoughts
Free from social boxes hold
Hoping valiantly to rise
To soar to heights where healing is
God's strength under my feeble wings
Who victoriously reaches heights?
Hidden in highest Hope is faith
To loose my chains and fly with peace

Tyrone Brown

Freedom

Prison walls have lost their power
Open gates - the imagination runs wild
No place out of bounds; no bars on the doors
Terror has fled at the sound of her name
Silence proclaims she is now in control
Under her flag peace overrules
Like an eagle she soars with the wind as her guide
Asking time to stand still as politely she smiles
Throughout her land there is contentment and joy
Morning dawns with sunlight's cheery warmth
No gray skies or storms of doom
In her garden of life the roses bloom
This queen is called "Freedom", and long may she reign

Lyndon Brown

Homelessness

Through the window the sights unfurl
Of life that passes in a repetitive swirl
Through the window he sees pain with its grip
Holding those hostage who have taken a trip
Through the window he sees homeless ones cry
For someone to care as they walk on by
Through the window he sees hurt and despair
That covers faces of the ones with no care
Through the window he sees hopelessness trap
The forgotten ones who fell through the gap
Through the window the scene is so dark
For those without homes that live in the park.

Lyndon Brown

My Mom

Her patience often tested
Her feet can go unrested
Her life's work is never done
Her children keep her on the run
Yet she gives her broken child
So much love that he has smiled
Councils him when things seem bleak
Wisdom from the Lord she seeks
Takes the time to play for fun
Praises him and says "Well done!"
Peace and safety she provides
To her all his fears confides
With her heart supports her son
Gives him courage life's race to run
Her gifts are precious as fine gold
They can't be bought; their price untold

Lyndon Brown

Positive Thinking

In positive thought we find relief
Knowing the value in faith and belief
Living in turmoil with frustration and fear
Life is so dark and nothing is clear
Mind with no power to fight negative thought
Down in the depths is where we are brought
In personal reflection we discover our fight
The war that's within, hidden from sight
Overcoming the enemy of anxiety inside
Erasing the hurt and despair, we confide
Our state of worry and pain within
To the One who will give us the strength to win
Trust writes words of hope in our mind
These are indelible, positive and kind
Overcoming chaos with order and control
Positive thoughts and there's peace in our soul

Tyrone Brown

Kolby

Rising star, protector and friend
Faithful companion, true to the end
With eyes of worship he looks for a pat
Then slowly turns to lie on his mat
The park his place to find a ball
With a sniffer so keen the tennis balls call
Soccer his passion he recruits us all
To play his game with the soccer ball
Tail wagging when he greets everyone
So happy to see you when your outing is done
Family he loves with devotion and care
Laying beside you on a couch or a chair
There never will be a Kolby so dear
The one so fluffy with long floppy ears

Lyndon Brown

Land that We Love

Land of freedom; land that we love
Efforts we make for the sign of the dove
Who will take this peace from our land?
Who controls values for which we stand?
This country is ours to serve and protect
Each one with a voice through those we elect
We choose acceptance of all social divides
Preserving our nation from sectarian sides
Remember it cost many their lives
Left mourning parents, children and wives
They thought our land worth dying for
They gave their all; they couldn't give more
This land of Canada stands hand in hand
United in peace; for freedom we stand

Tyrone Brown

With Thanks

Making progress is only found
In a place where care abounds
Through your gift of true belief
You give my mind peace and relief
Though many do not understand
Hard work from me is your demand
You find the way I can succeed
Then with encouragement proceed
Through all my times of tears and sighs
You help more than you realize
You speak in how my voice is heard
Bringing meaning to every word
Thank you especially for such care
Your consideration is beyond compare

Lyndon Brown

Nature's Portrait

Mountains in sunlight, with peaks in white pearl
The pictures of beauty begin to unfurl
Portraits of nature; the colours in view
Hearing the music of God's chorus anew
The birds, with spread wings, sore in tune with the sky
The canvas of blue stretched ever so high
Waters fresh pour through the caverns of time
Countless fountains fall, from the mountains in rhyme
Like hearts of red roses the pink flowers bloom
Their fragrance as a veil sweeps the valley at noon
Sunset paints its backdrop of coral and rose
As poetry written, natures wonder it grows

Tyrone Brown

Nature's Splendor

Yesterday's history is bathed in sunlight
Mountains of grandeur rise ever so bright
Beneath the cold snow, hard ice of years gone by
Glaciers lay with colour of heavens blue, blue sky
Rivers flow from highest peaks
With fountains of water into ice cold creeks
Great mountains and forests have such beauty to share
Places of nature with none to compare
Pacific Ocean salmon return with one goal
Their God given instinct is now in control
Place of completeness, life cycle goes on
Life will begin when the salmon are gone
Bears with cubs and deer with fawns
Countless wildlife rise up at dawn
The wonders of creation we view on in awe
Peace with tranquillity from this we draw

Tyrone Brown

Northern Reflections

In painted skies of wonder and light
The fingers of colour appear at night
Winter nights long with sun hiding from sight
But summer days linger with the solstice sunlight
Forests reflected in the waters so still
While streams of glacial water run down the steep hill
With wind underneath, the eagle's wings soar
Enjoying their freedom, the skies they explore
Writing a journal through time, rivers run
Finishing their story in the ocean when done
Noble mountains with snow covered peaks
Their statement of wonder and glory bespeaks
Reflections of greatness, beauty and light
Splendor of creation and God's hand of might

Lyndon Brown

November

The pumpkins are gone for another year
Our thoughts are now turning to Christmastime cheer
The fall leaves cover the grass with orange hues
With parting song, sparrows fly, bidding final adieus
Remembrance of the fallen will give all of us thought
Their sacrifice for country our freedom has brought
The days are now shorter, as the nights have drawn in
The weather much cooler as soon winter begins
With rain and wind, our plans are indoors
Warm by the fireside, as outside it pours
Reflecting on memories of warm summer rays
The tonic prescribed for bleak November days

Lyndon Brown

The Ocean

As purposeful as the hands of a clock
The endless waves crash on the rocks
Sending a spray with incredible power
Touching the sky with its salty shower
Pressing the sand with all of its might
Painting a picture; a beautiful sight
Applauding the storm with passionate spray
Washing the landscape almost away
Appreciating the moon overhead
Under its power the tides being led
Thundering proud the water portrays
Strength and fury with its awesome ways
Relentless waves, time only knows
Quiets our thoughts and calms our souls

Lyndon Brown

Our Strength

Wind whips the sand with power relentless
Rolling thunder growing louder through darkness
The lightning forks with dazzling brightness
Storms of life, with purpose our strength

Resounding waves in roaring splendor
These restless waves breaking rocks asunder
The power of the ocean full of greatness and wonder
Breath of life, God, His power our strength

With rain and wind the dunes will form
Plants will grow because of the storm
The sun shines down the ground will warm
Gift of life, with love, provides our strength

Lyndon Brown

Morning

Asking you to open your eyes
The morning comes with bright blue skies
With warmth, the sun beams with a smile
The day you hope will be worthwhile
As waking plants lift up their leaves
The birds sing songs among the trees
With softness of a downy chick
The alpine flowers grow full and thick
The mountain answers the morning quest
Standing tall, facing times great test

Lyndon Brown

Possibilities

Possibilities take flight when freed
The thought of hope is what they need
Winning battles fought in fear
"They'll never make it" is what they hear
Hiding deep within, is courage
To rise above those that discourage
Wholesome thoughts of choice to be
Not one with disability
But one who has something to give
With purpose found each day to live
In everyone is found a heart
That beats with hope, right from the start
Freedom has both joy and peace
Give their possibility release

Tyrone Brown

Raging Waters

Promise of storm, the dark clouds rise
Threatening tumult displayed in the skies
Powerful waves with thunder explode
Pounding the cliffs as the rocks erode
Torturous fury; the raging ocean vents
Wrath unstoppable until it relents
Untameable power, roaring its strength
No one can measure its breadth or its length
Over and over the waves pound the shore
Gaining control as it returns once more
Waters unleashed with magnificent force
Waters changing the shorelines course

Lyndon Brown

River of Peace

Meandering gently with calmness that speaks
Peace and gentleness to the mind that seeks
Rest from the rushing world all around
Ease and contentment, and natures hushed sound
With breezes sweet with fragrant wild flowers
The trees more vibrant from the soft April showers
In sentinel pose, the heron stands tall
High above in the branches, the black birds call
Rising out of the river, the rushes grow thick
Hiding provided for the water hen and her chick
Time seems to stop in this beautiful scene
With sunlight washing over the foliage of green
The river writes its journal through time
Giving the soul glimpses of the great and sublime

Tyrone Brown

Roaring Splendour

Returning waves in roaring splendour
With storm clouds fiercest darkness approaching
The wind driven water its fury unleashes
As the powerful ocean with its strength takes aim

The spray erupts with unstoppable force
Unbidden waves eroding the rocks
Relentless it pounds the cliffs and the shore
As the powerful ocean with its strength takes aim

Then on the horizon a ray of sunlight appears
The wind driven water calming once more
Waters of fury are harnessed with peace
As the powerful ocean with its strength is tamed

Lyndon Brown

Sounds of the Sea

Pounding waves in constant beat
This orchestra of nature will its song repeat
With symbols crashing as surf hits the shore
Percussion will lead the musical score
Rising above the powerful sound
The gulls as trumpets their calls resound
As flutes the sandpipers whistle on key
Their beautiful sound played in harmony
Wind with passion rises progressively loud
As the skies above gather black storm clouds
The music like concert plays in rhapsody time
The instruments of nature so hostile yet sublime
The conductor, our Creator, has composed the song
Nature's beauty and melody to Him belong

Lyndon Brown

From Darkness to Triumph

The darkness has control, with its grip holding tight
With chaos within, powerless to fight
Relentless winds of doubt and despair
The fear of wasting away without care
Reasoning thoughts can't find their hold
The rocks of self-worth are slippery and cold
Rains of disbelief in abilities pour down
Mind filled with pain threatens to drown
The raging river blocked by no way to speak
Without a voice; so feeble and weak
The storms of fear of pain become intense
Hiding peace and breaking hope's defense

Then through the storm brakes forth a ray of light
The beacon of trust; confident in ability to write
With sunlight convincing that home waits there
The warmth of devotion, love and care
The power of faith that God answers prayer
Having great peace; healing despair
The storm of pain gone with positive thought
Replacing with truth what negative brought
Confident hope shining light on life's way
Silence within; choosing calm through the day
Refreshing streams of strength, overcoming fear
The triumph of hope shining ever so clear

Tyrone Brown

The Ghost

Silent in the park he sits.
Perhaps someone will say "Hello"
This ghost is not invisible. He can be seen but no one stops.
Though having more hope than freedom to speak
He treasures the thought that someday he'll be
Given the chance to be considered by some
Why this ghost and why this pain?
Does society care he has no friends?
"Special" they call him - different his ways.
Do they shut him from view intentionally?
Despite his plight he smiles at those who pass on by
Few understand how cut off he feels
His ghostly state just becomes his life
Greet him with compassion if you happen to meet
His silence is not his choice you see
He's having to live on another path than most
But that path is lonely, when you are a ghost.

Tyrone Brown

The Social Outcast

The smile disguises the feelings within
The pain and loneliness felt again and again
His heart feels love, friendship and care
Yet reciprocal feelings from others is rare
Happiness hides from him, shutting its door
Society chooses his plight to ignore
The bar is so high for him to reach past
Who set the height for the social outcast?
Wanting an ear that will listen indeed
The longing with hope that he will be freed
Earnestly looking for respect with true heart
Not pity with sympathy, remaining apart
His journey through life as most would observe
Is threatened with social neglect and reserve
Hurting, with withering hope and despair
With need of a friend and someone to care

Tyrone Brown

Path of the Wind

Can its sound come through the trees?
Will the breath it has down leaves?
Where is it from and where does it go?
Does it say "You'll never know"?
Can we harness its might and power?
Will we make energy when it spins the towers?
Wind takes a path we don't understand
Invisible to us, yet it has the upper hand
The water will move whenever it blows
Under its power the hurricane grows
Having great might it does as it wills
Then when it's done, everything is still

Tyrone Brown

Power of the Wind

With power of an elephant roots are torn out
Evicting the trees and leaving no doubt
It has the force to take all in its path
Fling them in space, with a great aftermath
Wind has the way of destruction and harm
Raising its voice and giving alarm
But without being seen it soon exits the stage
Where silence is left where once there was rage
With a whisper it comes in the new day at dawn
Soft as a downy chick and quiet as a fawn
The leaves blow gently in the cool morning breeze
Its calmness so soothing, yet the wind no one sees
This power in nature controlled by God's hand
Has never been harnessed on sea or on land

Lyndon Brown

They Died Not in Vain

Freedom is the evidence of sacrifice and pain
Victorious in battle; they died not in vain
Embers still glow of their passion for right
Their fire for freedom for which they did fight
They gave unselfishly their lives for our land
With courage and valour they took their stand
With flames of hope the wars were fought
A blaze unstoppable, our freedom brought
Though winds of time have passed the years
We will remember their pain and tears
With silence they call us their torch to hold high
This message for freedom for which they did die
In gratitude we reflect on their sacrifice and pain
Victorious in battle; they died not in vain

Lyndon Brown

How Horrible the Marks of War

How horrible the marks of war
The homes that ever closed their door
On sons and husbands, only told
Destroy the enemy, be bold
They acted on their country's part
Home and family in their heart
They gave, unswerving from their cause
Today each one should stop and pause
To think about the lives they gave
Remember now those in the grave
In foreign lands, thankful are they
For Canada's soldiers on that day
Winning their freedom and great peace
May you and I then ask this piece
Do we appreciate now their pain?
Are we thankful for great gain?
The freedom in this land so dear
Belongs to us from all their tears

Tyrone Brown

Remember Them

Many wondered why they died
Could know the pain and tears they cried
They hoped this awful war would end
Their country on them did depend
Those soldiers could but wonder why
We know the reason why they died
For freedom we all have today
Valor and courage was displayed

Have we thought they died in vain?
Or do we contemplate our gain
They gave their lives for freedom's right
They fought amid the horrible sight
Of guns and death on every side
For this they did with country pride
Remember these they gave their all
Be thankful freedom was their call

The wars were fought for you and I
Beneath the poppies soldiers lie
For peace and freedom was their goal
Their families said it did console
Their death remembered through the years
How much they gave through blood and tears
More then the reason from this day
We owe our gratitude to pay

Tyrone Brown

Tyrone and Lyndon – Cultus Lake, B.C.

Little Brother

Little brother my best friend
The one on whom I can depend
In seas of trouble there you stood
The only one who understood
Without a word you spoke so plain
With intuitive eyes that knew my pain
Each road I travelled, you walked with me
Each mountain I climbed, I knew there you'd be
Giving me comfort by just being there
Our bond is so strong there is none to compare
Little brother, my best friend
On this you know you can depend

Tyrone Brown

Heroes

Those heroes gave all when they laid down their life
In past wars of this world with its turmoil and strife
The price for our freedom they paid with their blood
Their bravery was seen in the trenches of mud
Remembering our veterans and soldiers at war
The battles they fought; world peace to restore
Peace we should ponder in thoughtful reflection
The times in our past that brought fear and rejection
Our country is free because peace was their goal
They believed it was right with their heart and their soul
Our hope for future generations is a land of one voice
This hope is because they made it their choice
To fight for a world where nations agree
Where our country can stand in full liberty

Lyndon Brown

Canadians

True freedom our right as united we stand
Peace and safety our goal, across our land
Each Canadian proud of our Charter of Rights
Proud of our soldiers, bringing peace in world fights
With issues resolved by democratic vote
Our voices are heard without a doubt
Though some may try to spread their hate
With them we won't negotiate
As freedom appalls the acts of war
Greater our stand against what we deplore
As wars remembered, the lessons are clear
All that they bring are pain and fear
We stand united; we will not give
Peace must be ours for all to live
Thankful for those who protect our land
Canada our home, for which we stand

Lyndon Brown

Tomorrow

Asking what the future holds
Tomorrow will our dreams unfold?
The plans of something for our good
Praying we'll be understood
Surely time stands open wide
We trust our Lord to be our guide
Will we pass our song along?
Of peace and love, forever strong
The gift as we have all been given
Should be the master as we're driven
To ask ourselves what tomorrow will be
Will our goal be sure that we will stand free?

Lyndon Brown

Colours

Red and gold are giving a show
A performance of awesome colours that glow
Every season of autumn they display
Wonders of leaves in their fabulous array
The director, the creator, has written the script
This play will go on 'til the trees are stripped
We applaud the performers in the sunlight of fall
Expressing our delight they give us all
With the curtain of winter the act is over
Waiting for spring when life will start over

Lyndon Brown

Spring

Only Winter dresses in white and grey
Spring accents her wardrobe in bright array
The blossoms give the shade of pink
While hyacinths are the shade of ink
Reflective of her finery and style
The buds burst open with evergreen smile
Her lace which lines the land in green
With tulips embroidered, has to be seen
As a necklace of gold, daffodils grow
With raindrops like diamonds making her glow
Only Spring carries a bouquet to the ball
Arranged for her by the Creator of all

Lyndon Brown

Fall

Morning breaks so misty and grey
The rain descends on this cold fall day
Then through the clouds, with cheer the sun peers
Giving some warmth so the cold disappears
The changing season brings colours of red
With orange and gold leaves covering the flower bed
Something passes between summer and fall
Reflecting the changes that touch us all
Unspoken language of nature's timeline
With words that need no one to define
The autumn speaks of pumpkin and spice
The feeling of warmth that is always so nice
The ways of seasons we honour each year
Giving respect to their changes so clear

Tyrone Brown

Seasons

Looking at a tree, photosynthesis is clear
Summer with warmth, will make green leaves appear
Rains will water the roots in the ground
With wonder we watch beautiful fruit that abounds
The fruit bears the seeds; life is planted once more
Each year this happens as summer closes its door

Without a word autumn arrives on the scene
It paints red and orange, where once there was green
The gorgeous colours showing natures fine dress
On an artist canvas that will always impress
The falling leaves soon give end to the show
The leaves are gone before the falling of snow

Enter winter with long nights and the cold
Snow descends and with a blanket enfolds
The trees and the ground lay quiet and still
White woodlands cover the mountainous hill
Written as poetry with beauty and rhyme
Sample of God's handiwork and wonder sublime

Spring comes in as a guest to a reception
Another season a cause for reflection
With all of its glory in apparel of colour
The flowers bloom with a perfuming odour
Then out of the earth life of seeds will appear
The circle complete of the seasons each year

Lyndon Brown

Writing Waters

Waters write their names in the sand
With an inscription, that changes the land
As a witness to power, it signs "Erosion"
With waves that thunder as a great explosion
Words of greatest beauty recite
The poetry of the ocean's might
Sending its spray with incredible force
The air is filled with the ocean's chorus
The story is written in indelible ink
With power and strength never held by chain's link
Freelance writer of the shores of time
Its greatness speaks of God's wonders sublime

Lyndon Brown

The Journey Begins

In purpose it moves through the city streets.

The morning bright from the light of the sun, as a new day dawns.

Enjoying the sights through the windows rolled up.

There seem so many places to discover.

As it continues there are signs pointing the
traffic to popular routes to travel.

At the intersections there are stop signs giving it
time to reflect on the way it should take.

Purposely turning in the direction that will bring
success and joy it drives, speeding up as it goes.

Perhaps it seems there is nothing in the way but there are
potholes and bumps which suddenly stop it in its tracks.

Through perseverance it gets out of the holes it has fallen into.

The people on the street give a hand but it must help itself to continue.

At last it reaches its destination and in the rear view mirror it sees the
road it has travelled and realizes that it was blessed along the way.

Tomorrow it will start down another road and as an adult
pursue the success and joy it dreamed of in its youth.

Lyndon Brown

Ice Storm

Raining crystals, ice blankets the snow
With icicles hanging like ties on a bow
Though the spell that it casts, over trees and their limbs
Is like glass with small dimples, that encases within
Its prize that it cherishes shimmering in the sunlight
As diamonds and jewels ever so bright
Enveloped in ice, God's creation is cast
In a scene of serenity, but the spell will not last
Soon the ice melts, letting go of its prize
Cherished diamonds gone, as the temperatures rise

Lyndon Brown

Christmas Eve

Will it snow or will we get there?
Will we enjoy the fun that we share?
Christmas Eve a tradition which gives
Reflection of hope which in our heart lives
The family gathers with so much to eat
We inhale it all without missing a beat
With feelings of fullness from so many eats
We file downstairs and there take our seats
The carols of old we sing with our hearts
Prior to the little ones saying their parts
The evening is filled with laughter and fun
As stories are told of when we were young
Reason to celebrate we remember the one
Who came to save us; he was God's son
Christmas Eve that we wait for all year
A special time and treasure we hold dear

Lyndon Brown

Christmas

The tree is decorated with beautiful lights
The time of year of cold winter nights
The children are waiting for a special surprise
Excitement is seen in their dancing bright eyes
Friends come to visit and carollers sing
The songs of Christmas and jingle bells ring
Christ's birth we remember and the manger scene play
Bethlehem's stable and His cradle of hay
Pleasant hours we spend with our family so dear
Wishing all "Merry Christmas and Happy New Year!"

Tyrone Brown

Family Christmas

Yuletide songs with happiness ring
With family together we gather to sing
The table is spread with a feast to enjoy
There is laughter with cousins, with a feeling of joy
Remembering past Christmases, the stories are told
Presents that hold memories never grow old
Hope relayed of gifts under the tree
Gifts that are wrapped to you and to me
Some are planning to wake early at dawn
But parents say "No! Wait 'til the coffee is on"
Hearing the story of our Saviour's birth
How He came down from Heaven to earth
With His joy in our hearts His blessing we share
The time we give and show that we care
Christmas a season of love and good cheer
Ours is a Christmas we dream of all year

Tyrone Brown

The Most Wonderful Time of the Year

Under the tree presents are waiting
Wintertime cold means the children are skating
Carols are sung as we sit by the fireside
Jingle bells ring as we go for a sleigh ride
Time with our family means warmth with good cheer
Christmas, the most wonderful time of the year

Lyndon Brown

Christmas We Treasure

The house is strung with Christmas lights
In brilliance they light the dark winter nights
Wreaths on our door give a welcome to all
As friends and family come by to call
The tree stands dressed in gorgeous light
The presents wrapped will bring delight
Watching our mom bake our favourite treats
Making shortbread and tarts, filled full with mincemeat
The carols ring out their traditional sound
While we all are hoping for snow on the ground
This time of year with fireplace glow
The warmth we feel that just seems to grow
Christmas reminds us of our Saviour's birth
Good tidings to all and peace on earth
The season of joy, with giving and love
The time of blessings, that come from above

Lyndon Brown

Season of Christmas

Peaceful sounds as the snow softly falls
Songs of the snowbirds and the blue jays calls
Sprigs of holly decorated with snow
Voices sing carols by the fireside glow
Scenes of Christmas and the season of joy
Time to reflect on a sweet baby boy
This Son of the Highest who lay in the hay
God's plan for salvation He came to obey
Rejoicing, the angels sang "Good tidings on earth"
The Saviour with power to give second birth
Purpose of God, His gift to mankind
This season of Christmas, now hope we can find

Lyndon Brown

Music of Christmas

Each year it comes with anticipated joy
With happiness brought to each girl and boy
The sights of the season with voices in rhyme
Ring out to the world "It's Christmas time"
Snow surrounds the trees bright with lights
While carollers sing on the cold winter nights
Remembering the birth of God's blessed Son
Giving Him praise, as the angels have done
Peace and good tidings are sung out with joy
Sung with reflection of a sweet baby boy
We never tire of this season Hope brings
When families gather and everyone sings
This music of Christmas wishes happiness to all
Its songs as wings and the bluebirds call

Lyndon Brown

Christmas Chimes

Hearing chimes ring out with cheer
Christmas brings delight each year
Trees are lit with gorgeous light
As children gaze with eyes so bright
Sweeping boughs of evergreen
Across the mantles now are seen
The hearth is warmed by fires glow
The ground is white with winter snow
Wreathes welcome friends at every door
Shoppers bustling through the stores
Gifts from loved ones wrapped with bows
The feeling of joy in the heart grows
This time of happiness binds family and friends
With songs of Christmas our voices blend

Tyrone Brown

A Christmas to Remember

Christmas was coming but no gifts had been bought
There hadn't been work and hard times was his lot
So down on his knees, before his Lord he knelt
Praying for a miracle; telling the Lord how he felt
His children were hoping for a present from him
But without much money the hope was so dim
God heard his cries for a blessed Christmas day
Sending gifts to the door from dear Auntie Kay
There was a parcel of toys that each child was given
This was answer to prayer; a miracle from Heaven
To pray was his way and Heaven honoured this man
Special blessings at Christmas all part of God's plan

Lyndon Brown

Tyrone and Lyndon Brown

Purpose In Silence is a collection of poetry and devotional writings of two young men, who are non-verbal, yet have a voice through their writings. Motor impairment (Dyspraxia) and clubfeet have caused much frustration and pain in their young lives, but through these experiences their Lord has given them a deep understanding of His purpose for them and an ability to encourage others passing through trials. Faith in the Lord Jesus Christ is where their strength is found and it is the basis for much of their poetry. It is their heartfelt desire that their writings will bring honour to their Saviour and a blessing to all those who read their words.

Printed in the United States
By Bookmasters